WHAT PEOPLE ARE ⌣

"Erika Atkinson's innate sensibilities to this world, its inhabitants and all things beautiful, have produced a wonderful and inspiring book. With these stories, she has prepared a rich gift for all of us."
— Cathleen Gallander, Retired Art Museum Director, New York

"All boxes are checked. Erika is a super storyteller."
— Dee Spencer, Jazz Pianist, San Francisco

"Read her stories; they are what you get when you combine intelligence, wit, and grace."
— Cat Stevans, LGBT Event Coordinator, San Francisco

"Erika's open-hearted curiosity has for decades led her on whimsical wanderings and inquisitive encounters. Her stories enchant the mind, warm the heart, and inspire the soul."
— Andrew Gentile, Hypnotherapist, San Francisco

"Erika's intuition and clear vision are a convenient combination. Her approach to travel is a mix of curiosity, care, and a deeply-anchored sense of compassionate humor. These stories will inspire you to put on your shoes and start walking, to check for yourself."
— Gilles Jéronymos, Forestry Project Manager, Cadenet, France

"Erika is a master raconteur. She weaves a tapestry of far-off places and human experiences that compels the reader to turn each page with anticipation and fascination."
— Joseph d'Antonio and Marlowe Hyer, San Francisco

"Erika's travel experiences have been provoked by a variety of adventures around the world; they contain the kind of gems you go on repeating to friends long after she's already left for her next destination."
— Judd Kleinman, New Mexico

"Thoughtful and timeless, clever and wry, Erika's words show the exuberance of profound experience."
— Jacob Brownwood, San Francisco

HAPPILY LOST
IN TIME AND PLACE

BY
ERIKA ATKINSON

EXIT PRESS
SAN FRANCISCO

Happily Lost in Time and Place
Copyright © 2012 by Erika Atkinson

Published by EXIT PRESS

Cover Photo: Happy Hyder
Author Photo: Patty Nason
Book design by Richard Livingston

First Edition: May 2012

Additional information about EXIT PRESS at www.exitpress.org.

ISBN: 978-0-9774684-6-1

EXIT PRESS
156 Eddy Street
San Francisco, CA 94102-2708
mail@theexit.org

Posthumously dedicated to:

My Mother, who thought I might
My Father, who knew I would

. . . wander

CONTENTS

INTRODUCTION

Less than two years before the publication of this volume you are holding, Erika Atkinson, author and adventuress, committed the bravest and craziest act of her life: she stepped out onto the stage of the EXIT Theatre in front of eighty-plus people, and began to tell her story. That simple evening, entitled *A Tapestry of Travel Tales*, began an avalanche. Those five stories, handpicked from a half-century of traipsing around the planet, led to more. And more. While Erika has never been reticent to weave an entrancing yarn, she often underplays the vastness and the depth of her experience, rather like a woman saying, "You should see my chicken. It lays eggs," but who lets you discover for yourself that the eggs are Fabergé. What you are now holding is more than two dozen of Erika's exploits, each dazzling with rich golden prose and jewel-like insight. And we suspect there's more in the henhouse.

For those fortunate enough to have heard Erika read, there is a special joy to this collection. This long anticipated volume holds so many of the treasured stories that have been told piecemeal, over good cheeses and great bordeaux at extravagant hours, late and wee. For those who have not heard Erika read, and do not yet know her, there is a greater joy ahead: you may soon anticipate having a dear friend, both in the author and her work.

As with the best writers, Erika neither hides nor flaunts herself in her adventures — she is here just as she was when they occurred: simply and miraculously There. And simply being There, when it was right and necessary, has been Erika's incomparable gift for nearly all the years of her life. Her incredible openness and her ability to form connections (both intellectual and interpersonal) make this the antidote to all those travelogues saturate with posh hotels and prim encounters. Through Erika's crystalline vision, the dizzying whirlwind of humanity slows enough to show its heartbeat. Simply put, it is magical.

But, perhaps calling this collection of stories 'magical' does a slight disservice to its author. These are not tales of grand adventure astride the back of Providence. This is a smaller, humbler form of magic. Magic in the form of a Manitoba farmgirl playing with her prized possession: her father's globe. Tracing her finger along its curve and believing with all her heart that getting to the Antarctic was as simple as sliding on one's butt as far as the Equator, and then dropping the rest of the way. Though her progress was slower and more circuitous, when we finally stand beside Erika on the hoary rim of the subcontinent, there is no doubt to the reader that this is the act of a master conjurer.

Like the plumage of a rare bird, or the light of a distant star, these stories are but artifacts of a life brilliantly lived (including the lapses in caution and moments of freefall) — artifacts so fine and numinous in themselves that they summon in the reader a synaesthesia of surpassing beauty. The music of Chopin and raindrops in Mallorca; a crusty heel of bread and the eyes of a Russian grandmother; connections, once made, never to be broken. Oh yes, and Turkish bathrooms, too. So, perhaps calling this collection of stories 'magical' proves what any good traveler, writer, or reader knows to be true — that the most profoundly magical moments in our world are also the most deeply human.

It is with great honor and privilege that I introduce to you this remarkable volume of prose and poetry and, perhaps, a new best friend — Miss Erika Atkinson.

— Sean Owens
San Francisco 2012

LETTER TO THE READER

Let me begin with a disclaimer: though what follows could be called a partial memoir, it is ever so slightly fictionalized in some instances; but like any good work of fiction, it is all true. This collection of stories is a record of personal and individual adventures during my travels, not so much about locations, but about characters, situations, and experiences encountered in those places.

I have been traveling and wandering to remote and less remote parts of the world since 1957. For many years, countless friends and acquaintances have urged and nudged and encouraged me to share these unique experiences in published form. To publicize some of them has taken some courage, but I nonetheless offer you here a few of the many, for your entertainment, reflection, comparison, and enjoyment. I am certain they will conjure a memory or two of your own, perhaps a variation of the same story or location. All stories have been freely tempered by my imagination — the gap-filler between what I saw and what I felt, or perhaps didn't — which I consider to be the privileged sweet additive to the reality of an actual experience.

Travel is many things for me. Many stories in this collection are the result of coincidental but related events and happenstances, over a span of about five decades. Some of the stories carry symbols or signs that, when I recognized and acknowledged them, had a profound effect without knowledge of what that effect would be. I have never really been a madcap traveler; but I have always been a wanderer.

To all who have either read or listened to various of these stories, and taken time to comment after, I am deeply indebted. I have given due credit to sporadic quotations throughout the book, and for reasons of privacy, certain names have been fictionalized.

— Erika Atkinson
San Francisco 2012

I.
NOBLE SIGNS

SPARROWS BY THE WITTELSBACH FOUNTAIN

I was twenty-seven, and living in America, with an irrepressible urge to wander around the planet. To begin with, I thought I would live and work in romantic Old Europe somewhere. I was able to research some exciting possibilities, and very quickly decided to store all my household belongings and get on with adventure. I packed a sea trunk with a few improvised but necessary things, loaded it into the back of my brand new little BMW 1600, and drove to New Orleans, where I boarded a freighter several days later and was soon bound for the Dutch port city of Rotterdam.

By embarking upon this big first enterprise in the manner I did, I was cutting myself off completely from friends and family, I was leaving behind my life with no forwarding address, and I would have nothing in any of those categories to go ahead of me.

The ship, being a freighter, though allowing six passengers, had only one other traveler. Other than a box of Dutch brandy-filled chocolates and a stack of pulp fiction novels to amuse the day in a common room, it proved a somewhat tedious eight-day crossing. Escorted by a white-gloved harbor captain in his official greeting yacht, we inched the last kilometer, on a bright and sunny mid-September afternoon, into Rotterdam Harbor, one of the world's largest. My spirits were soaring.

The following day, my sea trunk and car were successfully lifted out of the ship's bowels. A sailor helped me load the trunk into the back seat of the car, we shook hands adieu, and I headed south along the beautiful Autobahns (freeways) of Europe, destination unknown.

I arrived in Munich two days later, discovering it was Octoberfest time, yes, in September. Being completely overwhelmed, a little weary, quite worried, and absolutely wired from the entire thirteen-day journey from home to here, I decided to stay. I was thrilled when I found my way to a hotel very near the Staatsoper, Munich's venerable opera house.

Walking about the city center next day, completely awe-inspired by this

Baroque capital of Bavaria, I came face to face at the end of a long boulevard with the giant fountain, the Wittelsbacher Brunnen, named for the Wittelsbach family, a European royal family and a German dynasty from Bavaria founded in 1180 and dissolved in 1918. Feeling empty and lost, I seated myself on its wide stone ledge and stared upward at this ambitious structure, astounded by its lavishness and enormity, also apparently a favorite photogenic spot in the grand middle of this very busy city. I had a little camera with me, and a curious passerby, wondering about me sitting there, came over and offered to take a picture. Thank goodness, as I now have a wonderful photo to remind me of an important moment of great value in my life.

While watching the water gushing and spouting, and sprinkling the occasional tourist with cool moisture, and being introspectively preoccupied with everything that had transpired in the past few weeks, I spilled over with tears, crying as softly and inconspicuously as possible. Doubt, fear, the unknown, not being familiar with a foreign culture, everything suddenly added up and consumed me with an overpowering melancholy. Literally everything I owned of any worth for this next while, including my little life-savings, was in my tiny duffle bag. I could muster only enough energy right now to sit here, and wonder, feeling quite forlorn, perhaps a little regretful, and even slightly stupid for such a rash decision on my part.

I pulled a cucumber sandwich out of my bag to enjoy a few bites. While munching on it, three little sparrows landed next to me, in obvious anticipation of a few bread crumbs. I naturally and happily shared a few. Two of the sparrows, completely oblivious to me, got down to the business of eating; the third stood there, all three inches of him looking straight up into my eyes. He chirped and chirped to me, for probably fifteen seconds, and then flew away, without eating a crumb.

To this day, I wonder what his message was, but I know what I wanted to believe it was. From his small but mighty perch, he was telling me to have courage, to have faith that things would work out. I just needed to shed doubt and let the sun back into my heart.

I ended up staying in Munich for nearly five years, enjoying one of the most incredibly enriching experiences of my life.

The Bread Lady of Haymarket Square

ST. PETERSBURG, RUSSIA
September 2003

I arrived in St. Petersburg on a chilly September afternoon and by prior arrangement was met at the airport by an English-speaking Russian couple who would be my chauffeurs, into and out of the city.

The long drive from the airport into the heart of the city, not surprisingly, proved a startling eye-opener for me: along Ñevsky Prospect, the main boulevard cutting through the center of the city, an army of rugged women, sweeping the street-side curbs and scraping away at corners with shovels and picks while flocks of shabby pigeons and a few rapscallion sparrows observed from above. I saw little elegance in the side streets, only shambled lines of one-room shacks and shanties painted ancient peeling blue, and scantily dressed children running in and out of them in bare feet, squealing with laughter.

'St. Petersburg', I said to myself, almost in disbelief, a city so far feeling eerily void and empty but also claustrophobic and crowded: empty buildings pallid and aloof, like monuments to dead dictators; crowded streets with scurrying citizens, impelled by inexorable darkness. No pleasure or ambition, only irresistible physical instinct.

My hosts delivered me to the apartment I was to call home for three weeks, just off the Haymarket Plaza, where Dostoyevsky once set his novel, "Crime and Punishment." In the muddy courtyard near the entrance to my flat, a savage-looking old reprobate lay on a soiled and torn mattress, eating his borscht with a proud snuffle, all the while uttering what I presumed to be caustic criticisms no doubt representing the entire metropolis of the common peasant man.

"Welcome to St. Petersburg," my hosts proudly announced.

The area may have been rich in literary history, but the apartment was dismal, considerably more so than I had expected, or even hoped for. Nonetheless, a set of large keys was handed over, a peripheral introduction given to each room, directions to dishes in the kitchen and towels in the bath.

In truth, the place was revolting, rancid with mildew and musty humidity. Sadly, a first glance around gave me an unsettling intuition. 'But,' I mused, undeniably lagged from thirty-six hours of coach-class travel, door to door, 'it is about adventure, about trust in unfamiliarity, about facing obstacles.'

Not to be daunted, I decided to head out into the fast approaching dusk to find something edible for next morning's breakfast. Stepping out the front door and under an archway that opened into the muddy Haymarket, I stood breathless and astounded as I stared around this foreign and microcosmic world.

Next to the archway, a solitary woman, whom I had not noticed upon arrival, was huddled like a sinister creature, looking like the last remnant out of "Crime and Punishment" itself. Upon sight of me, she got up suddenly and scurried away across the crumbly concrete.

Further along, in the middle of the plaza, I was astonished to see the number of kiosks selling only beer, vodka, and chocolate; nowhere did I see a stand selling a bit of bread or cheese, or even coffee grounds. Stunned into momentary confusion, I glanced about feeling utterly disoriented.

And then I saw her, just over there, by the side of another giant beer vendor, next to the canal: an elderly woman standing behind a square table with one leg missing, selling what looked to be the last half-loaf of day-old bread. From a few feet away, I watched her, all bundled in a greasy wool cap and sweater, tattered black pants and knee-high rubber boots. I couldn't help staring at her, bent with years of hardship, poverty, and aging. There she stood, at the mercy of the daily elements, steadfast in the chilled and moist evening air, rubbing her arthritic, blue-cold hands, while waiting with quiet dignity for a buyer to come along for that last remaining bit of bread.

Quite taken aback, I shut down my overwhelmed mind momentarily, shook myself into 'now', and stepped up to her table. I pointed to the bread with one hand, simultaneously raising fingers with the other to try to get an indication of the price — two fingers for two rubles, three fingers for three rubles — you get the picture. She raised one finger, for one ruble!

That's not even five cents, I quickly calculated!

Before I could intelligently summon my brain to its next action, I glanced closer at the lady, noticing very tired eyes set deep into her worn face. I wanted to reach across the table and hug her, hold her, and help her get warm.

Not having any Russian coinage on me just yet, I reached into my pocket for some of the paper rubles I had been able to purchase in San Francisco, and gave her five. A paper fiver! It was not my intention to placate — the first thing, I was told by a well-informed traveler to Russia, never to do. I just felt so bad for her.

The toothless baba, however, had her own set of standards. Reaching into a sooty old cigar box, she pulled out four coins and insisted on giving them to me. Extending her clasped black-knuckled hand across the table, I gently grabbed it in transit and gave her back one of the coins. I was playing with chance, but it was worth it for me.

She looked at me with the most genuine smile, when I saw a tear in the corner of each eye. I was teary-eyed myself, and filled with deepest emotion at such revelation: people who have endured poverty and suffering all their lives, and managing nonetheless to continue standing tall and proud — a first close-up view of something very Russian, old Russian, desperately Russian. I had just become aware of one more meaning for gratitude and grace.

Accepting the half loaf from her, I bowed slightly in respect, and sidestepped to the canal to reflect beside it a moment. Looking along its full length to where it made a bend up ahead, my eyes were prompted to look upward, toward a sky glowing red from a beautiful sunset somewhere. I was elated, and just as I was about to thank the muses for guiding me to this weathered old soul behind her bread table, I saw one of the things that had brought me to St. Petersburg in the first place — way down at the end of the canal, a towering golden onion dome atop a Russian cathedral, reaching half-way into the red sky, for all the world to see.

I gathered my composure to walk back to my flat, but not before glancing over once more to the lowly bread lady still folding up shop. For me, she was the true Russian monument. She became instantly carved into my mind, a memorial to all the grace that could possibly be reflected in the splendor of one golden dome hanging high above Russia. Like a fabled halcyon, she had calmed the winds of my mind and warmed the autumnal cold waves in my heart.

Just before heading back to the flat, I stopped at the largest kiosk in the middle of the Haymarket Plaza and purchased a small bottle of that Russian fire several friends had told me about.

I promise you, day-old bread dunked in the purest distilled vodka never tasted so good!

I just needed to make sure I had enough leftovers for breakfast next morning!

II.
COGENT COLORS

Pour Vous, La Grande Bleue!

COLLIOURE, FRANCE
September 2002

you lap close in
you rush far out
     to sea
you hiss as you weave between jetties
you roar against salt ships
     and beyond distant sounds
you surf consistently
you are there
     always
          for ever
and then you are gone
     now
          for a while
you are the old Has-Been
but remain the mysterious Will-Be
     Was
          Is
               Shall-Be
you churn gray with mist
you bubble up against polished sand rocks
you whisper into the cracks of concrete piers
you rise up against the horizon
     swallowing
          my secrets

into your immense well

a stranger from halfway around the world
　　i visit your shore
　　and you magnetize me
　　　　hypnotize me
　　　　　　greet me
a stranger
　　i came
a nurturer
　　you welcomed me
　　you covered me
　　　　while i slept beside you a minute
　　　　on your time-worn stone bed
　　you stood guard
　　　　proud
　　　　silent
　　　　no breath of wind blew
　　　　　　where i slept
i dreamed i was a single moment
　　in a single day
　　　　in your single sentry's stance
momentarily you swam away to the horizon
　　but returned
　　　　gray
　　　　obscene green
　　　　luscious see-through blue
　　　　brown
　　　　purple — soon
your eastern horizon appeared speckled
　　with little gray imperfections

suddenly turned into white perfect sails
there you were
    in the now
        gone turquoise
        even gray
        returned coral blue
        sky blue
how are you so calm returning
    while so busy?
    sombre-ness
        today
    sun
        another
    moonlight
        soon
    yellow reflections
        now
        from lime green mountain edges
            and dark olive brown ridges
behind me
    spotted stone walls of arabic origin
before me
    little blue boats
        with brush-stroked orange ledges
        and painted red bench seats
    washed white sides
        with ancient names etched in black ink
a lighthouse bobbing ahead
    whistling with rust
    singing a symphony of sounds
        adorned by color

    painting a picture
        with the noise of the sea

dusk is coming
daylight is leaving
    drawing definitive horizontal lines
        on vertical promises
        while i dream
            with a capital D

and you
    chère la Grande Bleue
        are like the helium balloon
        registering the rise of warm
            the fall of moist
            the air going hot and cold
            seldom any normalcy between

thank you
i am now seeking the sign that says
    this way to heaven
    and it points to Collioure!

WAITING

AMSTERDAM, HOLLAND
June 1996

luscious tall girls
in narrow cubicles
glowing skin
ravenous brown faces
skimpy laces
waiting
      for the door to open
dark marble eyes
peering out of the glass
at some guy's ass
the look that lures him
into her universe
invites him
to drop a few florins in her purse
the look unduly wise
the look through the red light haze
the gaze that knows

looking from the inside out
she knows what her world's about
through piercing eyes
expectant eyes
sad eyes
young old eyes

hands that know how to move
hands that know the groove
waiting
      for the door to open
wishing
      hoping
           wondering
                standing
                    waiting
for the door to open

ADONIS AND THE LESSER GODS

MUNICH, GERMANY
December 1979

After leaving a wonderful life in Munich, I hit upon the idea seven years later of a pilgrimage back. I felt a strong desire to return once more and walk through many memories of a life that had become such an important part of my personal history and makeup in the late Sixties. I remembered that the dead of Winter in South Germany is not unpleasant. It is picturesque; it is like stepping into a snowy postcard. So, I did just that, and after celebrating the fantasy and fairytale of Christmas in Bavaria, and visiting several friends here and there in Austria and the Tyrol, I finally returned to Munich itself for New Year's Eve celebrations, a bacchanalian night I would never forget amidst the hundreds of revelers and merrymakers.

I had purchased a ticket to participate in the traditional Sylvesternacht Abend (the New Year's Eve celebration) in the renovated caves under the Rathaus (City Hall), and it promised to be a highly animated evening of dining, drinking, and dancing. Before too long, I discovered I was sharing a table with two distinctly different German couples, one South German and very cosmopolitan, the other North German and very provincial, which would surely provide a decent amount of paradoxical dialogue as the evening progressed. The South husband was a chemist of international renown, while the North husband was a renovator of historical homes, restricted to the confines of Hamburg. Artistically, I knew from past years, one could generally find most Europeans agreeing; historically, they sometimes agreed; but politically, they never agreed! As the evening continued, the North and South could not even agree on whose beer was the better, never mind politics. I remained the silent observer and made no attempt to mediate the on-going arguments. Disagreement was inevitable and as natural as the moon in the heavens, and I smiled to myself, thinking, 'Oh well, the New Year has been appropriately and officially greeted!'

Midnight had come and gone, with great and appropriate fanfare, and once again, another New Year had begun. As far as I was now concerned I needed to leave as it was getting close to one o'clock in the morning, when trains generally stopped running. I went over to hug the waiter who, earlier, had given me a little black chimney-sweep doll and two tiny pink ceramic piglets, both symbols of good luck in Germany — which, he assured me with some devious pleasure, had been given that evening only to single attendees. I smiled, pleased, and danced off into the Munich night.

I surfaced from the bowels of City Hall, and a concierge, strategically placed at the exit, informed me, much to my chagrin, that trains had stopped running one hour earlier on this night. I was flummoxed and confounded. Suddenly the German logic made no sense whatsoever and seemed completely irrational. And taxis, something to be coveted on any late night in Munich, were few and far between, particularly in the big pedestrian middle of this big city. So, this being New Year's Eve on top of the dilemma, I had no choice but to give in to the moment and go with the flow, and this left me beautifully primed for the muses to take me where they desired. Already just having surfaced onto the Marienplatz, the main square, was enough to make my insides melt; it had turned into a veritable Winter wonderland up here. I was overwhelmed at the beautiful sight. There was the ancient Mariensäule, the Virgin Mary and patron saint of Munich, mounted high into the darkest heavens on her pedestal. I paused for a moment to reflect on the fact that, all World War II memories of this famous square aside, this evening, like a grandiloquent watchwoman of history, she seemed to cast a tranquil mood upon the people passing beneath her, in this great city of consequence at the foot of the Alps.

Right next to the Mariensäule, in all its own splendor and majesty, stood the symbolic Christmas tree, a giant, all lit with thousands of tiny little white electric lights — I wondered for a moment if at one time they may have used candles for this traditional tree. I stood below, leaning in sentimental silence against a gas lamp, glancing down side streets, alleyways, and walkways. No roar of car engines passing through. Only stillness. And out of the inky black sky above, big lazy snowflakes tumbling indolently downward, gracing with their perfect geometric shapes whatever surfaces they landed upon. People, all in their festive array, out to celebrate this night, arm in arm underneath outstretched parasols, criss-crossing the cobblestone plaza, acknowledging and bowing to one another, an inveterate but consistent and concise manner of the aristocracy of the city, part of the normal social order of its citizens, the simple perpetuation of centuries of esteemed and formal etiquette.

Everything seemed so grand and ornate this evening. An ancient decorated city still feeding upon its past. Vintage gaslights, all in perfectly measured lines, were casting a slightly opaqued haze upon the entire setting, reminding me somewhat of a French Impressionist painting — but definitely in three-dimensional motion on this festive night! It was time present set in time past. It was now, inside long ago, or was it long ago here, and very much present?

A tremendous feeling swept through me; this evening was a special gift to me, as I stood leaning against the same gaslight, looking, staring, watching, remembering, and being translocated, being permitted to traverse the impermanence of something very permanent. Stunning evanescence!

Standing firm in this wondrous night of nights, a rush came over me. In my long black velvet evening coat, adorned by my then almost waste-long silver-blond hair, I even dared myself to feel singled out for something unique this night. By myself, alone, in the middle of this city I had loved so much and whose pulse I had learned to feel with great comfort all the years I lived in it, I was thrilled to stand here, in the heart of Europe, far away from home, far away from anyone who knew me or knew what I was doing, or where. No one knew me who passed by. This was my moment in my history, my moment in my life. This was my gift to me, part of the evolution of my own mythology, my privilege — to see it all, and feel it all, and try to comprehend the magnitude of its silence and beauty, its grace and nobility, somewhere in a reverie between Id and Ego, between the dream and awakening.

Beginning to feel a sense of hypnosis setting in from the night's chill, I began contemplating a move toward the train station when very suddenly, out of the mist and to my left, I noticed strolling straight toward me a solo male figure, very tall, very smartly dressed. When he got closer, I could see his handsome face: translucent olive-toned skin, and big black eyes set deeply behind rather pronounced and perfect eyebrows. In this gray-white snowy setting he became the perfect Adonis! I stood completely still against the gas lamp, my hands in my coat pockets for warmth, and watched him with great intensity, if not curiosity. I was quite captivated. In fact, I was transfixed by his convergence. The closer he moved towards me, the more intensely I stared at him. Looking straight into his face, I discovered his unrelenting gaze upon me, accompanied by a sweet half-smile. For a few frozen non-threatening seconds, we locked in upon ourselves, a moment I suddenly hoped would never dissolve. For what seemed an eternity, he stood staring, absolutely face to face with me. His warm hand came slowly out of his pocket, and he raised it softly to my face, gently touching my cheek, asking: "Gnädige Frau, erlauben Sie mir, Sie zu küssen?" (My Lady, allow me to kiss you!")

Very calmly I tilted my face upward towards him and, pointing to either side of my face, I responded: "Gerne! Wie Sie wünschen!" ("Yes, as you wish!"). He kissed me ever so delicately on both cheeks, then looking once more steadily into my eyes with a pleased smile across his face, he turned and walked away. Completely mesmerized, I watched him disappear, until he was fully absorbed by the darkness of this memorable night. I was left, standing against that gaslamp, feeling pure euphoria. What an unbelievably exhilarating gift! It was not imagined.

Way up on her pedestal, the patron saint of Munich was smiling down to me. She knew about such things . . . in fact, she had probably caused them to happen this night!

~ ~ ~ ~ ~ ~ ~

Unfortunately, the endless warmth in my heart was not able to curb the chill that was slowly but surely creeping into my bones. Trains had of course stopped running, presumably to begin again at five o'clock in the morning, and taxis were nowhere to be had or found. Left with one choice, I began a slow plod to the train station along the main boulevard on foot just to keep in motion. And so began a long and cold winter night's ride of another kind.

I recalled from the years I lived in Munich a warm waiting room at the back of the train station — small but always heated, a room mostly being used by transient middle European workers and laborers who had been brought to this land of plenty to build city undergrounds, to earn some of that 'plenty' to send home to wives and children, mothers and mothers-in-law, in Greece, Yugoslavia, Turkey, and Armenia. The idea of heat at this point in the night was extremely inviting, and so I kept walking. A little faster.

Eventually I arrived at the station, but found to my great dismay and disappointment that the entire front of it was now locked, closed to the nighttime transients. Could this really be? Could this really be the same train station? Once the harborer of the lost and hungry and cold wanderers, now locked up tight! No longer a warm haven for the forlorn and weary travelers, who depended rather heavily upon the temporary hospitality of wooden train station benches for beds, and the corner twenty-four-hour pretzel stand for food during endless waiting hours for trains back to their homelands!

Not to be daunted, I knew this temporary discomfort would not be a permanent dilemma for me, and in the interim, something would evolve, helpful, interesting, or both. I had crossed paths with seemingly impossible obstacles a time or two in my life, and I was well familiar with uncomfortable challenges now and then.

Walking along the edge of the front of the station, I discovered several hot air registers sending up plenty of warmth. Standing on top of one of them, I was no longer questioning anything, as I felt the welcome warmth flowing upward through me, gradually easing out the over-all chill. Within a half minute of being there, another 'soul of the dark night' sidled up to me, and while I was willing to share my warm spot with him, I was not willing to respond to his obvious search for more than just heat from the register. I was not inclined to shatter the image of my earlier glass menagerie moment on the square and so passed up the hint, politely, suggesting he might try to pawn off his discontent on the next handy mortal, just one hot-air register over.

With feet at last sufficiently warmed, I trundled around to the back side of the station, determined I could somehow still get inside, and find that heated room I remembered. Trying several doors along the ledge, one finally opened, and I had found the room, as crowded and smoky as always. I entered, hearing nothing but intermixed noises of foreign languages. I couldn't keep from squinting — the room was literally blue from the smoke of Turkish and Brazilian cigarettes! Through the haze, I could see at least two signs, in German, on the walls: "Rauchen verboten!" ("Smoking prohibited.") It was my guess the inhabitants were quite able to read German, but more than likely decided they deserved their perks for the New Year's Eve as legitimately as anyone else.

I found a vacant spot on one of the benches, next to an old grandmother all dressed in black, holding a tiny infant all dressed in white. Across from the grandma stood a very handsome Greek, perhaps Yugoslavian or Turk, wearing a thin beautifully embroidered cotton shirt, the only piece of clothing covering the top half of his body in this cold winter night, unbuttoned to his navel, and his hairy chest proudly displaying a gold religious medallion. He was sending rather crude vociferations across the room, trying to 'make time' with a young lady, who looked quite haughtily disinterested, dressed in her purple hat with a wide brim. Every time the man opened his mouth to say something, the grimacing grandmother next to me turned her head in shame, embarrassment written all over her shriveled and time-worn face. Behind me, a very drunk gentleman was having great difficulty in his inebriated state balancing his limbs on the edge of the chair being so 'generously' shared by the corpulent lady next to him.

Time flew by in this 'live theatre.' When I next glanced at the clock, it was, gratefully, a few minutes before the gates to transportation and liberation, not to mention the first day of a brand new year, would finally open again. In preparation to board the train, I ambled down the escalator into the underground, perused the schedule, and . . . to my astonishment and utter horror, found that trains would not be running a normal schedule, due to this being January 1st, a holiday day. My train was leaving in one more hour and I immediately became at least twenty-five degrees colder!

There were a few benches down here in this dungeon for use, but they were plastic and so very cold to sit on. So, I walked, up and down the platform about twenty-five times. When, after a while, I grew tired of pacing, knowing that the bench would add at least another ten degrees of chill to my fanny, I went in search of the warmest spot! Down at the end of the platform I noticed a bench with a very heavy-set man on one end of it, and on the other end, a pair of lovers in 'warm' embrace. I loved the prospect. Sitting in that spot between the over-sized man and the lovers, about an eighteen-inch space, would be just enough to keep me warm if I could squeeze between them.

I wiggled in, trying not to disturb either side of me, and succumbed to the instant warmth surrounding me.

The train eventually came. By seven o'clock I was home. I never enjoyed a hot bath more in my entire life. Even the marrow of my bones seemed frozen. Crawling under those big European featherbeds in my friend's bedroom was the most pleasurable indulgence of my journey. I buried myself in them, and within minutes I was fast asleep. As for January 1st of 1980, I do not remember it, but when I arose later that evening, I thought: "So I missed one day but why be concerned when a whole new decade lay ahead of me."

~ ~ ~ ~ ~ ~ ~

[In the Summer of 1999, I was back in Munich, sitting on a bench in the English Gardens, pondering that entire long ago event. A little trumpet band marched by, jarring me back to the now. Today, on this warm June day, the sun was pouring out of a very clear blue sky. I got up, plodded ahead, toward the Marienplatz, semi-consciously in search of my Adonis of the long ago night. Nowhere to be seen, I strolled along the big and wide and wonderful commercial Neuhauserstrasse, which all those Turks and Greeks back then had helped build above the new underground. I passed by the Michael's Kirche, toward the Stacchus which once was an enormous empty round hole, endlessly deep. It was the big vortex for the Munich underground system. Above it, waters spewed forth from a fountain, newly designed and safely nestled inside the moon-shaped plaza I had crossed so many times thirty-five years ago. I finally reached the train station. No evidence here either of any long-ago frozen cold night. All station doors were open and all trains were running, on time.]

III.
WINDS OF
TIME AND PLACE

I GROW UP ONCE

MANITOBA, CANADA
October 2011

i grew up once
never thought i would
never thought i wanted to
just a prairie girl
demure then
but curious
always dreaming
under my maple tree branch
stretched out on a summer blanket
looking skyward
communing with clouds

the summer prairie girl
i remember her well
she wrote her secret on a leaf
wrapped it inside a bigger leaf
and buried it
the leaf decomposed
but the secret never did

the winter prairie girl
i remember her well
hating the frigid blizzard winds
howling through cracks
of a non-wind-proof house

windows frozen thick with ice
nothing to see
nowhere to go
except back to my cold corner
of a room where we all lived
and learned that six times nine was fifty-four
and much more of that
from where i wondered if my snow-laden branch needed a hug

doldrums drove me to find something to read
in one of dad's three books
or a country guide magazine
where i fell in love with the picture of a dog

i melted a tiny hole with my breath
and my finger
into the ice on the windowpane
and there i saw it
horrid winter
a fencepost covered with a giant snowball
the little summer pond frozen solid
and icicles hanging from my beloved branch

i wrote on a piece of paper
i want to leave this place
when i'm grown up
i want to go somewhere far away

and i did

A Dare

I was asked by the Dean of Creative Arts at San Francisco State University to consider an intriguing, if challenging, four-week assignment in Taipei. The Creative Arts School, together with the National Taiwan Academy of Arts, was planning to organize a weeklong conference, bringing together regional and international experts and professionals in art history, fine arts, music, design, and so on. This was to be called the Asian Pacific Conference on Art Education (ASPACAE), under the theme of "The East Meets the West in the Arts." Fundamental differences in teaching would be discussed in hopes of leading to ways to bridge the gap between the philosophies of Eastern and Western cultures. My duties would be multifarious, including everything from translating presentation papers into English (from German and French), to organizing the logistics of flights and hotel accommodations for guests and participants coming from around the world.

It was during the organizing and planning of all this that the President of the Academy, my administrative supervisor, said one day: "Erika, when this is all over, I think we should plan to take your American guests somewhere on a one-day trip of special interest and curiosity."

I immediately gave him a somewhat insouciant response: "Yes, Quemoy, the nationalist stronghold island on the edge of mainland China!"

Rather surprised, he said, "Fine, interesting choice, and we'll try to organize it."

Quemoy, today known as Kinmen Island, would be the last place on earth I would ever visit in my ongoing normal travels, but I thought since we were in Taiwan why not do this. I got nothing but enthusiastic responses from my fellow Americans.

~ ~ ~ ~ ~ ~ ~

Quemoy was a small archipelago of several islands administered by Taiwan, the Republic of China. During the late Fifties and early Sixties, the island had been the site of extensive shelling between forces of the People's Republic of China (mainland China) and the Republic of China (Taiwan).

The 1960 presidential election campaign between Kennedy and Nixon came to bear on this unrest as well when, in the Fifties, the United States had threatened to use nuclear weapons against mainland China if it attacked Taiwan.

As recent as 1981, Quemoy was still a military reserve and holdout against mainland China, therefore making this a not-necessarily-safe excursion. It would require two low-level armed military reconnaissance jets to escort us there and back, and thankfully President Cheng, with his connections throughout Taipei, was able to choreograph that.

Thirteen of us registered, and flew to Quemoy in a twin-engine twenty-five seat clunker airplane. The jets on either side of us were not visible, nor did they land on Quemoy. But we did, and quite safely, disembarking directly into a long and dark tunnel, along the entire length of which fully armed policemen and soldiers were lined up for our protection. Their guns were not aimed at us, of course, but I will admit to feeling some claustrophobic fear walking through that tunnel.

Once we surfaced at the other end, we had entered the large tower called Juguang (which translates into 'brightness of light'), a famous landmark on the island. It was, in fact, the only doorway onto the island for pedestrians at that time, and as such, a rather non-descript building, whose interior was mostly jade columns, with nothing furnishing the space other than a customs check stand. We all got through and were free to wander about for two hours.

I was suddenly not interested in military museums or war history, so I turned left and went off to a seaside shore to sit on the sand and watch the beautiful Chinese junks sailing on a very tranquil China Sea, actually the Taiwan Straits. It was a very soothing view, and inspiring for me while I sat there with my journal, writing thoughts onto the pages about the entire experience I had just had in Taipei.

Just before returning to the airplane, I strolled through some of the ancient alleyways between old jail cells, noticing in particular the deep trenches in front of these cells that had served as toilets for the prisoners. Poor China Sea, I thought!

Before sundown, we were flown back to Taipei, and I was rather pleased at having made this suggestion. In flight, one of the passengers said, "Erika, we missed you at the museums."

I smiled and said, "I am sorry, but I was happy to watch the Chinese junks sail on the gentle sea. I'm not particularly interested in military museums displaying killing instruments."

I had read about this island that in recent years local Quemoy artisans had collected vast amounts of exploded ordnance and military shells, from which they made high-quality knives, still sought after today by chefs and food connoisseurs around the world. The island also had a famous brewery that made a very high-percentage alcohol called Kaoliang liquor, 38 to 63 percent alcohol.

~ ~ ~ ~ ~ ~ ~

Had I known before takeoff that morning what a foray into a republic of fear this would be, I'm not sure I would have so blatantly suggested it. But I liked the word "Quemoy" and was curious to know what this historically sinister place was all about.

As noted, Quemoy today is known as Kinmen, a frequently-visited national park. It was returned to civilian government in the mid-1990s, and since 2001, travel is easily permitted back and forth. It is a peaceful location known for its quiet villages, its old-style architecture, and its warm sandy beaches.

Fifteen Minutes in Solitary Confinement

EPHESUS, TURKEY
May 1994

I had just enjoyed two weeks of wandering on the Greek island of Chios. Sadly, it was time to leave its idyllic and peaceful isolation, and move on to my next destination: the ancient Greek city of Ephesus, now an anthropological restoration site in southwest Turkey.

On the morning of departure from a very small island port, a timeless and stalwart fisherman helped me and one other traveler into his creaky moss-rimmed fishing boat, recently motorized, he proudly assured us. For about an hour, we drifted through relatively calm Aegean waters, zigzagging between other islands and peninsular outcroppings, eventually being safely and harmlessly delivered halfway down the west coast of Turkey, at the resort city of Izmir — a rather flat and treeless place undulating in steaming Summer heat with a population of more than four million inhabitants.

We disembarked and were immediately greeted by two armed guardsmen at the customs checkpoint, neither of whom seemed in any way willing, much less prepared, to help anyone. Observing the scene around me, I recalled the disconcerting feeling of seeing yet another foreign and, for me, unreadable language. Albeit colorful, signage everywhere looked more like mardi gras posters than directions to post offices or banks.

I inched my way through the customs checkpoint and saw a sign with what looked like a dollar bill drawn on it and an arrow beneath it, presumably pointing to a bank. I followed the arrow and it did indeed lead to a money kiosk where, in exchange for one fifty-dollar traveler's check, I received a wheelbarrow full of Turkish money! The exchange value was something like three thousand lire for one dollar. Thank goodness I had a canvas bag, folded inside my travel bag, though not necessarily intended for 'emergencies' such as this!! I also realized at that moment why the clerk was so annoyed with me — he must have just given me every last paper lire from his vault!

A few steps beyond this money depository, I noticed a rather desultory local leaning against a terra cotta wall, apparently without aim or ambition. I challenged him by asking for directions to the 'autogar' — the bus terminal. I needed to get to Selçuk, a small town near Ephesus. The gentleman complied most affably, and I headed happily into the unknown, but hopefully toward the bus terminal.

The mission was accomplished and in not too long, an elderly turban-wearing gent boarded the bus, took his place in the driver's seat, and started up a sputtering engine. Several careening maneuvers and lurches around sharp corners, a few narrow weaves through backstreets cluttered with dogs and children, and we were at last on what are called highways in rural west Turkey. Rumbling and bumping along, by now fully succumbed to the discomfort of no air conditioning, I realized that the phrase 'highway to hell' had just taken on a whole new depth of meaning.

A grueling bus ride, to say the least, from one coastal extremity to another, but we arrived, on this very hot and dry day, apparently still several kilometers from the edge of ancient Ephesus! For unknown reasons, and I didn't know the language so I couldn't find out why, the driver insisted on dropping a few of us in the middle of what seemed like nowhere, near the only tree in sight — a very old and noble olive tree, thick and bent and twisted with time — on a stretch of road, next to a village which I guessed to be a small suburb of small-town Selçuk.

Wandering toward the village in searing midday heat, I came upon a tree stump and, half lethargically, decided to sit down and survey the situation for a moment. In the near distance and alarmingly noticeable, a grotesque box-shaped gray concrete structure loomed three stories high, punctured here and there with gaping glassless windows. It seemed entirely like an optical illusion in this environment as I looked at it in disbelief. 'The building must surely have been intended for a correctional institution,' I mused.

It was at this point my body was beginning to send a certain very familiar signal. I had drunk a large bottle of water during that interminable bus ride, and I suddenly sensed an urgency to find a public restroom facility.

Feeling somewhat abandoned and alone, even though surrounded by a colorful abundance of indigenes, I advanced across a path toward a one-room dwelling in front of which I had spotted three young men engaged in lazy banter in the burning afternoon sun. Realizing I was in Islamic country, there would be no local women in sight. And this was a small primitive village, which meant there may not necessarily be public facilities to accommodate women, since not that many tourists were even about, at least not walking alone like I was in the middle of this day.

It was the only time in my life I would have preferred being a man so I could easily have left my discomfort behind that old olive tree — no disrespect to tree or man!

I approached the three gents, put down my little travel bag, and with gritted teeth and crossed knees, made a gesture they easily interpreted. All three tried to hide a snicker, nonetheless respectfully. One of them took the lead and motioned I follow him. Walking obediently behind him, I suddenly realized with some horror, we were heading straight toward the entrance of that large ugly concrete building which, up closer, loomed even larger and uglier. Once there, he pointed me up the stairs to the entrance and left me to my whims.

Seldom daunted by too much that concerns travel adventure, I walked with reasonable confidence up the five steps to two enormous doors. Seeing no code boxes or intercom systems, I simply tried the door. Not entirely to my surprise, it opened! I entered, and was certain I had just become an illegal trespasser — or a prisoner?

Once oriented to the deafening stone silence within, people voices became faintly audible off in some eerie distance. Stepping cautiously across this big empty room toward another door at the opposite end, I opened it, only to see that I had entered one more empty room.

I froze, beginning to feel fearfully claustrophobic, not to mention trapped, in this desolate and gray vacuum filled to capacity with void.

In an attempt to gain control of my disquietude, I stood there no longer than fifteen, what seemed like interminable, seconds, when suddenly the door across this room slowly opened and out came an official who appeared to be of some importance — he was wearing one of those traditional forest-green police uniforms!

I should normally have been at least a little apprehensive, but the desperate needs of my body had become too acute, depriving me of any ability to concentrate on anything beyond that most crucially at hand.

The officer approached with about five deliberate steps, his official and stern demeanor completely intact. When he seemed non-threatening, I moved a step toward him and offered a handshake — which he acknowledged with a rather rigid nod of his head. His hands held behind his back, he remained silent, all the while studying the expression on my face. With a furled brow and wrenched smile, I very emphatically spoke six words I insisted he would understand: "Sir, excuse me, emergency; a toilet?"

A half smile emanated from him, which I took to mean he understood. Still not speaking, but with some dignity, he motioned for me to wait a moment, while he stepped back into the dimly-lit room from which he had entered earlier.

Through the open door, I could see a large desk, with two of those gaping windows behind it, which I had already seen from the outside. The officer reached up to a large brass hook on the wall, upon which hung what very much looked like a jailer's turnkey, attached to a grooved miniature log. He removed the entire contraption and then motioned me to follow him even further into the bowels of this colossal building.

I followed him, through another door, and up a very long flight of stairs. We walked straight ahead a few steps and then turned a corner, which led directly toward a dead end. There I could see what appeared to be a huge industrial-sized door. The officer went right to it, inserted that big piece of metal into an apparent keyhole, turning it once this way, twice that way, and with appropriate creaks from rusty hinges, a three-inch-thick steel door opened.

I could no longer deny it — sudden fear, significant anxiety, and not only slight bewilderment, had now killed my curiosity completely.

The officer turned to point me inside, almost as if to say: "It's all yours, lady!" My well-bred upbringing could not prevent me from bowing slightly in passing, to thank him.

Upon entering this ominous room, an unbelievable stench greeted me. I lowered my head and stood frozen in timeless and silent space. The silence, however, was quickly shattered when the door slammed shut with a vengeance behind me, creating a bang so loud it vibrated and echoed throughout the entire hollow building. I jerked forward and was, I feared, surely locked in for life.

But no time to worry about rotting in a tiny musty room in Turkey just this second. The necessity to do something to take away nature's pressing pain became increasingly urgent.

Looking around in semi-darkness, I saw nothing immediately that I would recognize as a toilet. Furthermore, the only light into the room came from one long and narrow six-inch slit in the concrete wall at eye level, making this place look altogether like the interior of a Carthaginian fortress. I nonetheless inched bravely ahead — and finally saw it: the infamous small sunken brass hole in the floor, all of eight inches in diameter.

No problem, I shrugged. I was, after all, a well-trained farm girl who had grown up without electricity or plumbing on the bald and windblown central Canadian prairies.

Relieved at last, and put back together, I decided to try my luck with the tiny water spigot I noticed to my right — it produced no more than three drops of water in five seconds, by my count. Next to this faucet, I was amused by an empty plastic Evian water bottle with the top half cut off, whose intended purpose, I laughed out loud cynically, surely was not to rinse off the brass hole. And otherwise, I was not about to leave any gratuities here for anyone.

Finally reasonably intact, I stepped cautiously and fearfully back toward that thick steel door, suddenly reminded it might have locked me in, accidentally, or not. Reticently, I pulled the handle and to my enormous relief, the door opened! I wasted not a second stepping outside, waiting once more for that same impact while the door slammed shut with all its might behind me!

Finding my way out of this unbelievable building was like walking through a maze, but some by-gosh turns and a few calculated guesses brought me miraculously back to the main double doors, where I could, at long last, end this cell-block tango and exit to freedom. While the ancient architectural sights of Turkey thus far had dazzled and amazed me, this building had only puzzled and dazed me.

By now, I had just enough time left in the day to get to my destination — Selçuk near Ephesus. Taxis being very prolific, I crawled into one nearest to me. The only thing I could say in Turkish was the town's name, where I seriously hoped to find a hotel with a bed, in a private room, but without a three-inch steel door separating me from the rest of the world.

Within minutes, the taxi driver delivered me to The Hotel, right on the periphery of Ephesus. For his kindness, I paid him at least one inch of paper lire, and stepped out into the sticky heat, feeling overwhelmed once more by the pressing crowds — peddlers, hawks, dealers, beggars, muezzins, pushers, and taxi pimps — frantic above the din of tinny old secondhand cars speeding uncontrollably down a few dusty roads.

Here meanwhile, in The Hotel, in my small room with a small bed, and a small toilet, and a small basin, all was forgiven.

I opened the shutters to see if I might catch a whiff of ancient history, and screeched with delight: directly in front of me were the remains of five Greek columns, each standing sentinel to what may, at one time, have been part of the outer wall of Ephesus. And to my added delight, each column had a stork's nest upon it, with one or two babies romping happily; a lovely chatter to fall asleep by!

In the reasonably cool early dawn of next morning, I headed at last into the rutted marble streets of ancient Ephesus. Upon first glance, the collective of restored ruins did seem a little like unidentifiable jumble, festered and crumbled over the millenniums. But in the midst of it all, I managed to find my way to the top of the semi-restored amphitheatre.

Here, in a wide open space, in the full glory and splendor of a still-cool morning, and far away from yesterday's temporary imprisonment, in vaguely remembered words of Jan Morris, my most-loved travel writer, I pondered the ancients of Ephesus from one of the most historical places on earth: "Hawk-nosed sheiks bickering flamboyantly; political exiles engaged in unceasing deception; poets and artists exchanging visionary discourse; unkempt existentialists in frayed sandals proselytizing; and doe-eyed women from Constantinople smiling wisely by the side."

FINDING MESTA

CHIOS ISLAND, GREECE
October 1994

A rare non-miasmic day provided the perfect mid-morning setting for departure from old Athens on an Onassis-owned Olympic Airlines flight, across a teal blue sea toward the island of Chios. Reclining in a luxuriously comfortable seat on this relatively small but upscale aircraft, I reflected with great satisfaction upon all that I had seen and heard the past ten days in the anthropological heartbeat of historic Athens. I thought back to the very early morning I stood with awe at the foot of the Parthenon, sending up exhortations to Athena, the great goddess of wisdom and divine intelligence. I remembered with special pleasure a few animated dialogues over coffee in the Agora just below the Acropolis, with two English-speaking Greek university students, the 'frail saplings', as Henry Miller called them, drooping on overload with all the wisdom they have inherited by virtue of the fact that they were Greeks living in Greece.

In my research and preparation for this journey, I had come across a compelling description of Chios, the fifth largest Greek island in the Aegean, just five kilometers from the Southern Turkish coast. Besides appearing to be remote and charming, and definitely far less traveled than most other Greek islands, it was described as a fascinating enclave, particularly with its completely intact medieval villages, one of them being Mesta, which had been built in the Third Century B.C. as a covered maze for protection against Aegean piracy, and which was still well preserved.

I exited the little Olympic flying machine and cleared passport check in a breeze. Outside the terminal, a clanky shuttle bus, with room for five passengers, took us less than ten minutes away to the edge of the small town of Chios, dropping us at its reinforced wharf lined with small storefronts, information kiosks, and a few arts and crafts boutiques.

Stepping out of the minivan, we were all instantly met by the customary onslaught of aggressive taxi drivers, one of them managing to more or less lynch me and quite literally lure me into his cab. It took only thirty seconds and a half kilometer to realize he was more of a highway robber than a genuine cab driver — the kind I had been warned about in the travel guide. I was indeed caught off-guard, and very quickly an uneasy feeling began to sweep over me.

Babbling something uninterpretable for me, the driver bolted like a shot out of a canon, racing off with me, his hostage, forcibly confined. I realized he hadn't even asked me where I was going, much less let me tell him in the first place, so we could haggle for a best price. I tapped him on the shoulder and, with the most forceful sign language I dared to use, demanded that he let me out onto the quay. With his rattly little car spewing exhaust fumes in all directions, he kept speeding further along the narrow one-kilometer ocean quay as if he was on the longest speedway in the world! I tapped his shoulder again, and yelled: "Monsieur, arrêt! Stop!" Midway between nowhere and nothing, he slammed on his brakes, bringing the poor dilapidated car to a screeching halt, and there he waited, impertinently, while I exited the car and deposited myself on the runway. He dared to turn around only once to glare at me with subversive eyes. I shut the car door with a loud bang, leaving him inside the vehicle waving his hands and uttering a string of obscenities equivalent, I'm sure, to anything that qualified for 'dumb tourist' and beyond!

Feeling momentarily bewildered by a fiercely belligerent taxi driver who had just managed to rattle my equilibrium rather mightily, I took a look around me, trying to assess where I might be in this sleepy little seaside town. It was approximately midday.

Gradually a feeling of calm set back in, and it was in that moment Dame Fortune, as if waiting in the wings, smiled benevolently upon me. I spotted the agency that had been listed in my guidebook as a car and motorbike rental depot, and doubling as a travel information center. Many months ago, I had contacted this agency via letter from home and, albeit in cryptic English, fallen into a good old-fashioned diplomatic business correspondence with a human being named Costas Chandris, an amiable and enterprising young man. I stepped inside and met him, face to face, telling him I was the one from San Francisco who wanted to rent a little three-wheeled roadster. He convinced me after some discourse, however, to get a certain four-wheeled jalopy he had in mind for me, a fancy covered go-cart, that he assured me had been well maintained and would be the safer and more advantageous transport across the rough gravelly roads of Chios island.

All the paperwork completed, I asked him to point me in the direction of Mesta, the village of my destination, the place in which I had chosen to spend my time for a week to ten days or so.

"Ah, you are going to Mesta?" he said, his eyes lighting up. Stepping back into his office momentarily, he came back with a map, saying: "You will enjoy Mesta. It is on the other side of that mountain," he pointed, toward the southwest. "Just follow the road, only one road. It is an hour from here and not difficult to find. And when you are there, madame, you must ask for my friend Dmitri Petitas. He knows everything about this unique place. He will help you find a room to live in, and he will take care of you."

I smiled broadly, and with no small amount of satisfaction. Dmitri Petitas was the person I had also read about in my faithful guidebook, which had described him as a colorful local character, and though living in Mesta, he was notoriously well-known across the island, honored and much-loved as a kind of benefactor in many ways, revered almost as a god by everyone who knew him, and that pretty much included the entire population of the island — which was about twenty thousand people. The guidebook had assured me that mentioning his name was like summoning magic in an instant, and in that moment Dmitri would appear to offer assistance as needed.

Armed with great feelings, plenty of enthusiasm, and elated to have fallen into the capable and guiding hands of Costas, I settled into my trusty little four-wheeled buggy. With one short stop at a small food vendor to purchase a few bottles of water, and a few victuals and edibles, I left the town behind me as I rattled and sputtered and clattered down the dusty road, on my way at last to the other side of the mountain, perhaps even to a first sunset on the Aegean, if I was able to maneuver this little put-put with a bit of expertise and confidence.

~ ~ ~ ~ ~ ~ ~

It all began with thirty initial kilometers of driving and bumping across rugged terrain, through incredible countryside. Here and there crude huts with a door and two windows, belonging to no time and no place, made me feel I was on another planet. I loved the primitiveness, the rugged beauty, the stiff shrubs looking like porcupine quills, sporadic bald patches of clay, a few clumps of wine vines, pockets of semi-fertile land isolated from one another, and colored with bursts of wild flowers and butterflies. I could feel my heart singing in the semi-arid landscape of this far-off place of light.

Following the one road to Mesta, per information from Costas, I suddenly came upon a puzzling fork in the road, and no signs with directions, or even arrows pointing. Contrary to Costas' simple instructions, I now needed to make a decision, or at least guess correctly. I turned right, since that felt more like southwesterly, the general direction in which I was going, and soon ran into a little village a few kilometers down that road.

"Mesta," I thought, with screeching delight, even though there was not a sign in sight to indicate anything of the sort.

I stopped when I saw a wizened old man sitting on a lone chair in front of one of the façades along the main street of the village. "Mesta?" I asked. He waved his crooked finger in the negative, then pointed further southwestward along the road.

Of course it wasn't Mesta! It wasn't a covered maze. But it was quaint and obscure, and eerily uninhabited.

A few more kilometers down the road, I approached another village without identification, and I was thinking I'd love this one to be Mesta; in fact, I was convinced it was — perfectly medieval, and beautifully intact. When I slowed to a stop, spotting an elderly gent with bushy eyebrows sitting on the stoop of his blue-doored entrance, I again cried out through the car window: "Mesta?" He, too, shook his head in the negative, and pointed in the same direction as the previous villager, showing a deliberate hand with five fingers, indicating what, I wondered. Five kilometers, five minutes, five more villages down this bumpy old road? So I was still not in Mesta! I was so eager to find Mesta, that I kept forgetting it was a covered maze with a center that I would ultimately be walking, not driving, to. Where I was now was a slightly larger, regular open air village, and I was obviously driving through its center.

Getting out to walk a bit, I came upon two little pottery shops, and wandered into one of them. A sudden sprout of human activity forced its way out of inertia in the form of a beautiful about twenty-year-old woman, who spoke a little English, and told me this village was Olympi, one of five mastic villages of the island. Mastic, I had read, referred to the tree from which a kind of chewing gum was made, which, she said, the Greeks loved to chew to whiten their teeth.

I browsed around for a few minutes, bought a tiny painted clay cup from the young woman , and then, while I still had the momentum going, I hopped in my bantam car and pushed onward down this seemingly endless road to Mesta.

At the end of the main roadway through Olympi, I finally saw a sign with an arrow, but no words. I turned where the arrow directed me, and in just a few more kilometers, another village did emerge, a very quaint little place, and my mind was convinced, this was Mesta. There couldn't be much more road left beyond here, and the seaside was approaching.

Driving slowly forward and slightly downhill, I was fascinated by the unusual designs on the house fronts, painted in small checkered and diamond-shaped motifs, in all colors imaginable. Another remote and secluded village but, it then hit me once more, not a covered village. Out of curiosity, I inched along to where I spotted a bent and elderly woman sweeping the street with a twig broom. She paused and slowly turned her head toward me, naturally recognizing me as a stranger. Once again I called out of the car window: "Mesta?"

She nodded her head in the negative. "No Mesta!" she exclaimed empathically. "Pirgi, Pirgi!" she said, smiling a vibrant toothless smile. Then with her contorted right hand, she waved rapidly southward, saying "Mesta! Mesta!" I thanked the venerable lady by tilting my head and doing a kind of silly but respectful salute and kept moving. I sensed she had a bit of humor in her, especially when I noticed her watching me through the car's rear-view mirror.

Meanwhile, I was beginning to feel I was running out of island. There couldn't possibly be much more road to go, and there didn't seem to be any sign whatsoever to another village, either down the hill or around the bend in the road. Mountain footpaths abounded, a few sheep and goats were grazing, and gnarled and crooked trees, which I suspected to be the indigenous mastic tree, were evident in commendable clusters.

~ ~ ~ ~ ~ ~ ~

Noticing a beautiful twilight slowly beginning to envelope the island, meaning I probably had about an hour left before dusk completely descended, I remained undaunted as I watched the sun's orb turn into a red hot coal at the horizon. The sun was sinking behind the sea, and the vital spark of adventure in me was definitely rising. Alone in my world and my fantasy mind, I fully expected the hesperidian goddesses dressed in golden light to join my evening's frolic at any minute. It truly is impossible to watch a sunset anywhere and not dream or desire. In the best interests of my wandering spirit, I decided to park my little car alongside the roadway next to a dried up olive tree, turn off its raspy engine, lock the doors, and settle into my driver's seat with my journal as I watched dusk fade into night. A few hours of rest would be good for me after that drive, and I was already intrigued with what a new day's dawning might reveal in this enchanted place.

~ ~ ~ ~ ~ ~ ~

Before darkness descended completely, I wrote into my journal:

I am in a peaceful place on the planet. No sparring natives or warring nations can possibly interfere with the pristine serenity and calmness I am feeling as I watch an evanescent panorama of color on the horizon fade into darkness, and bring out one million stars to play in the elegiac skies above the Aegean. I am remembering back to my youthful days of dreaming the undreamable, lying under my favorite branch of an old tree behind my mother's notorious potato garden, where I was taking imaginary running leaps and vaulting into the blue bigness, floating like an angel in the air, and flying about my secret sky whispering joyously to the clouds.

Here, on this gnarled mountainside of Chios Island, I am at last experiencing some of that youthful euphoria.

~ ~ ~ ~ ~ ~ ~

Early next morning, continuing in my journal:

A dawn is awakening me from a temporary slumber as it spreads its rosy fingers across the sky. Stepping out of the car, I feel what a privilege it is to be here, alive, breathing, thinking, observing, and absorbing all of it. Morning, the best time. Vapors rising from the earth. Night's dew clinging to thistle plants and making them glisten.

The sun is about to burst into the sky behind me and turn up the day's temperature. For now, in this semi-arid and deliciously warm place, I hear a few small birds warbling from several thickets, calling one another. Whistling beetles are feasting among the prickly greens, and busy bees are already at work inside acrid though colorful blossoms.

It is momentary perfect happiness.

~ ~ ~ ~ ~ ~ ~

And so, I had a great sleep in the seat of my little car! Stepping out for a good morning stretch, a splash of water on my face from the plastic bottle, a mouth rinse, and I was ready to forge ahead. Believing that the elders in all the previous villages would not have steered me in bad or wrong directions, I set out with a firm conviction that I was now very close to my destination.

I had gone three kilometers at most along this dusty puzzling pathway when a beautifully painted wooden sign came into view just ahead. "Mesta", it said, in ornately carved Cyrillic lettering, with just enough symbols similar to Latin so that I could read it and know I had, at long last, reached this mysterious place. From a distance of perhaps one hundred meters, I could see a small rather non-descript and uninteresting place with broken terra-cotta-colored outer walls, seemingly overgrown with contorted trees. There were no individual buildings, just this big earth-colored odd-shaped structure near the seashore. With a modicum of consternation, I whispered to my bewildered self: "This is Mesta?? Why does it look abandoned and empty?" It did not look anything like the rustic stone fortress I had read about, seen pictures of, and fantasized so much about back home.

In a safe first gear, I headed slowly along the same road, now even narrower, which led me toward an entrance that seemed to be a gateway to this impenetrable place. The only direction I could turn, once inside the gate, was left, and continue down a tiny alley that wound in a semi-circle towards the right, barely wide enough to accommodate the width of my little car. I assumed, not to mention hoped, it was a one-way lane, if it was a car lane at all! I inched along but nothing seemed to be stirring anywhere, until a few surprised villagers poked their heads out of glassless windows, looking quite bewildered.

A few hundred feet ahead, still on the edge of this strange building, I came to a sudden clearing, thankfully with some room to better maneuver my car and park it next to a wooden fence, beside a harnessed mule tied to the same fence, who showed no sign of alarm when I did so. He didn't even budge. Behind the fence was a a small garden, a cabbage patch, in fact, and next to that, a wooden hut, presumably the residence of one or two locals. And a short distance beyond the hut, off in the near distance, a very blue-green sea, whose shore seemed but a few hundred steps away, the sky above wide-open and cloudless, and the mid-morning sun beginning to beat down. Perhaps the inhabitants had not yet awakened for the day. Whatever I had stumbled upon, I was beginning to see that it was a perfect picture-book scene of oldest Greece, timelessly set in one periscopic frame.

Not seeing any sign of life so far other than the mule tethered in suspended stance next to my little car, I felt inspired to put on a sun hat, pack my water bottle and my journal into my shoulder bag, and head down the path that led me directly to the shore of this beautiful sea.

I found the perfect place to sit and listen to the hiss and foam of the surf, at that junction where, as Walt Whitman said, "the solid marries the liquid." Here, on the blue-green shore of the beautiful Aegean, I watched the sea sparkle in the midday sun, in the ambience of solitude and the sand, and I had no wish to change anything or be anyone else, even be anywhere else.

~ ~ ~ ~ ~ ~ ~

Reflecting on Pablo Neruda's poetic love of the sea, I paraphrased, to the best of my memory, his sensuous words into my journal:

> *here alone*
> *only the waves of the sea speak to me*
> *i don't understand their mutter*
> *as they move and withdraw*
> *i can't hear their whisper*
> *as they seep into the sand*
>
> *here*
> *time is obliterated*
> *i can only listen to its richness*

~ ~ ~ ~ ~ ~ ~

I'm guessing it's going on early afternoon as I stroll back to my car. Convinced

I have at least reached the outside wall of Mesta, I'm happy.

I also realize life is two things here: slow and quiet.

~ ~ ~ ~ ~ ~ ~

I was leaning against my car, strategizing my next moves, when as if out of a mirage, a peasant appeared from the hut. I watched him as he hobbled in my direction with a confident gait, a long gnarly stick in one hand to help him with a slight limp. Presumably he was coming for his mule, but he bypassed it and kept walking to within a few feet of me. Assuming he didn't speak English, I quickly and quietly arranged some mental sign language to prepare for the imminent exchange, for I did want to ask if this was indeed Mesta, and if so, the big burning question, 'How could I find Dmitri?'

I had barely begun gesticulating when I saw a young man, who I guessed to be his son, come out of the same hut, followed by a woman, coarsened and bent with age and heaviness, carrying a large garden shovel. Both ambled toward the mule, where they waited patiently for their master before taking their next steps. With some slightly hyper signage on my part, the dialogue began; a colorful colloquy indeed. Big smiles became the adverbs of the conversation, and the gent and I made eye contact knowing, I think, we would understand one another well.

"Mesta?" I finally spoke out loud, pointing toward the earth-colored enclosed hamlet. And to my joyful relief, he nodded his head in the affirmative. I folded my arms across my chest to bow a thank you, and he smiled broadly, his old teeth completely tobacco-stained. I then dared to take the plunge and utter one other word: "Dmitri!"

As if I had mentioned the most beautiful word in the world, his silent face lit up completely, and I suspected he had, in that same instant, become immediately aware of my needs. Dmitri was that guy who was supposed to help me find whatever I needed anywhere on the island, which for now would hopefully be a room in which I could stay for a week, somewhere inside that maze.

The farmer began moving his arms in all directions, and immediately drew the young man into the 'conversation'. A few moments of whispered counsel between them, a nod of approval from each, and the young man left, disappearing behind the wall of the maze. The veteran peasant looked back at me and signaled what I easily guessed to be: "Wait here! Dmitri will come, he will come!" I bowed in thanks, and went to wait next to my car, while the woman was given permission to go back inside the hut for now.

The old gent, during this interim, leaned himself across the little wooden fence, as if in a quandary about his cabbage garden. He could see the damage a few rabbits had done during the night, and looked back at me shaking his head, mystified.

Within minutes, his young emissary returned, completely animated, chattering loudly to his father, who gave him a sweet pat on his head. I interpreted from his ensuing sign language that I was to follow him and his son in my car. They would walk in front of me, while I drove very slowly behind them to just inside the wall of the village, and into a space under a roof, which I could see was just big enough for two very small cars. It must have been recently and newly arranged for the occasional wanderers on wheels such as I was.

I stepped out of the car into a sudden drop in temperature, and the delicious smell of cool earth. My heart was pounding with excitement because I finally realized I was about to enter this covered medieval metropolis, and walk with these men through the maze to its center, where I presumed I would at last meet the great god, Dmitri Petitas.

The three of us set off. I wanted to stop everywhere and look, but they had a mission to fulfill on borrowed time, and I needed to keep up with them. Many turns and corners, past fascinating entries to the tiny dwellings of the inhabitants, past aged peasants leading their donkeys laden with supplies along very small stone cobbled alleys under vaulted roofs, in semi-daylight. And then we were there, at the center of this fabled place, where there actually was no cover, but where there were two bistrôts, each under its own canopy, and a small church whose steeple pointed beyond its tiled roof directly into the blue sky above.

The farmer and his son invited me to sit at a table on the edge of one of the bistrôts, motioning for me to wait, and then they disappeared back behind me to a shaded side, but within sight of me. There was not a soul to be seen anywhere. It was the eeriest feeling I'd had in a long time, here in the middle of an ancient village, on this very remote island, thousands of miles from home. It must have been siesta time for it to be so quiet.

While I waited, I looked about with awe and wonder. The village of Mesta, the guidebook said, was the most distant of the medieval villages and also the most well-preserved. I could finally see the unique architecture I had read about, the living quarters built very tightly and side-by-side all throughout, with only two entrances to the entire village, on opposite sides. The alleys, one of which I just walked along, covered with arches and vaults, were just wide enough for one-person two-way traffic. At ground level, slanted toward the center of the path was the trough for water drainage, or a place to dump waste water, perhaps. A village built as a maze — an intentional structure to prevent the raiding pirates of old from reaching the most important buildings located in the center of the village, or even from entering the village at all.

Just when I had settled into a medieval frame of mind, gazing in wonder at this awesome structure, the farmer's son burst from the shadows toward my table, pointing in a great frenzy at a gentleman looking out onto the plaza from a second-story window. A very handsome Greek, I thought, looking to be about sixty years in age. "Dmitri, Dmitri!" the farmer's son uttered in a half whisper, pointing with great excitement in his direction. Dmitri and I spotted one another, so I decided to wave up to him, and he responded in kind.

The farmer's son hastened back to where his father was standing in the shadows, and in less than a minute, the sagacious Dmitri had descended, and come to meet me at the bistrôt table. "I am Dmitri," he said. "Welcome to the island of Chios, and to Mesta!" He then side-stepped to shake hands with the farmer and his son, who seemed utterly excited about this big and unusual adventure in their day. They disappeared back along the vaulted alley, and Dmitri came to sit down with me.

"Welcome!" he said again, and before he sat down, he asked if I would like a cold beer. He spoke very good English, I noticed immediately, which seemed so oddly out of place in this remote location.

He gave a semi-shout, in English with a definite Australian accent: "Despina! Bring us two cold beers!" and within minutes, a very attractive young Greek woman wearing only scant clothing, a sleek long ponytail, and a rather petulant attitude, emerged from the darkish interior of the building next to us. We were introduced, and I had no doubt she and I would become much more familiar with one another over these next days! She, too, spoke English.

Dmitri and I chinked bottles (no beer glasses in this place!) and in moments he asked: "So, how may I help you?"

"Dmitri," I said, "it is so great to have found you, and you seem every bit as wonderful as the guidebook says you are."

"Thank you," he said. "I was not responsible for that description, but it obviously works." He was smiling from ear to ear, with all his genuine enthusiasm in place. A thoroughly modern man, I thought to myself.

"It's such an unexpected surprise to find you, in a completely unknown place, so far away from my home, just from the mere mention of your name in a travel book."

"Very few have been as lucky as you," he smiled, and I loved that comment.

I wanted to know how he had come to speak such good English. He was thrilled to tell the story: "It's the Greek marines," he said. "They have taken me to many corners of the world, and I spent several years in Western Australia. As well, I still travel to New York every now and then because I have a grown daughter there! But for now, I am the self-proclaimed Mayor of Mesta, and I enjoy it very much," he said, looking altogether pleased. "I love to show this unique little village to the few visitors who have come from so far to see it."

"Dmitri, will you help me find a little room to stay in, hopefully here inside the maze, for about a week? A small space inside the wall of this enchanting Byzantine stone and mortar village would make me so happy!" Of course he would, but first he wanted to show me a little more of its quaintness.

I was fully enchanted by this alluring labyrinth of very narrow, twisted, tiny lanes and worn walkways, low-beamed arches looming overhead, supported by mud-brick walls of a hundred earthen colors. Dmitri walked me through, waving to all the shawled women hanging out of their windows, eyes glazed from years of hard living, a few of them having animated conversations with one another across the alley. We walked past a doorway which had a small mule tethered to it: "Private taxi!" Dmitri joked with a big belly laugh. And hoisted up across the alley, thin fig tree branches, strung with white linens drying in the gentle breeze.

We were walking down a pathway which had a dead end, and Dmitri explained: "That is the outer wall of the village, it is four meters thick. Now watch carefully. We will turn right into a little foyer, and here behind this entrance," he said, pointing to a round-topped heavy blue door, "will be your home for as long as you wish to stay."

I was ecstatic. A large brass key opened the round-topped door, and allowed me to enter into a vaulted room directly inside the outer village wall, completely white-washed, with a few stones protruding here and there from the wall, providing a bit of rustic decor. I stood in breathless stupor, trying to inhale the emanations in one swoop. Dmitri was amused. Swiveling on my feet in the middle of the room, I stretched my neck right, left, and upwards, to take it all in, to smell the earth, and to wind the gears in my mind way back in time.

A short wooden bed stood in one corner with a brilliant-colored woven wool blanket atop a very thin mattress, and there was thickly carved old furniture sporadically situated throughout the room. There was even a small cooler for the traveler's benefit. "That was installed," Dmitri explained, "with part of the money the Greek government once gave each island for maintenance and 'home improvements' such as a tiny kitchen, and this modest shower stall, with a sink and toilet nearby."

Dmitri then walked back with me, diagonally across the village square to the South exit, where my car was parked in 'the garage'. He helped me carry my larger bag, and once deposited in my room, he bid his adieus, and said: "Welcome to our old village. Please feel free to yell from the platias up to my window if you need anything. If you are shy to do so, Despina will do it for you!" I laughed out loud, knowing Despina would be considerable cause for fun and entertainment throughout this stay.

I spent a few minutes setting up my little room, and was about to head out into this labyrinth, to do my first test walk through, when I saw Dmitri coming back in my direction with a bottle of chilled white retsina and one stubby stemmed wine glass. "From Despina," he winked. "She likes you!"

~ ~ ~ ~ ~ ~ ~

Overjoyed and filled with eager anticipation, I locked that big blue door behind me and strolled toward the square, managing not to get lost along the way. Of the two tavernas, I chose the one I had been in this morning, on the far side which, Dmitri had whispered to me, was his favorite of the two. It was, in fact, owned by the lively and fearless Despina. The other taverna was run by Stavros, an old-timer from the village, a somewhat cantankerous gent, whose not-so-pleasant antics, Dmitri promised, I would have ample opportunity to observe.

After this day's rather arduous adventure, I was ready to sit down under the canopy of Despina's tavern, and enjoy the balmy evening under this Grecian sky. Beautifully painted ceramic pots bursting with red geraniums were hanging everywhere. Despina, noticing me from her kitchen, came along in her colorful attire. She was definitely the only woman in this village not wearing the customary black dress, long or short. Tonight she was wearing a bright red sleeveless tank top, and white shorts, impeccable accents to her healthy olive-colored skin. Her beautiful long black free-flowing hair created a perfect frame around that glowing face with its piercing brown eyes, daring anyone to duel with her.

"Nice to see you again," she said, as we gave one another a warm handshake. "May I offer you a glass of wine or a beer?"

I was so impressed with her knowledge of English, and eager to hear her story as well. "Thank you, yes, I would enjoy a chilled white retsina. That would be great!"

Bringing back my carafe on a tiny wood platter, with a piece of goat cheese and a small piece of crisp toasted bread on the side, she sat down to join me for a while to, as she said with her mischievous smile, "Practice my English!" With that, she poured my wine, offered the Greek yiamas (cheers), and sat down.

"Despina," I entreated her, "tell me about yourself. Where are you from? Where were you born? How did you get here? I am very curious about you. Please forgive me, but you seem out of place here!"

With one corner of her mouth turned up into a half-smile, she beamed: "Oh, you really want to know? First of all, I am the owner, manager, supervisor, and head cook of this taverna. It once belonged to my father. It is in honor of my father that I have kept it running; otherwise, I would not be here."

Leaving no doubt behind, she also gave me a very distinct feeling that she was the indisputable head mistress of this village square. "And I have a family here with me," she said, pointing first to an absolutely angelic boy, sitting on a small stool against the tavern wall next to a tall green mastic plant in an olive oil can. "That is my little nephew Alexos from Pirgi, the village you came through on your way here. Alexos has volunteered to help me this Summer in exchange for food, lodging, and experience." The boy and I made eye contact as he sat there listlessly snipping the ends off green string beans. I smiled first, and he smiled back somewhat reticently.

A moment or two later, Despina's two daughters arrived on the scene, chasing each other, squealing with healthy laughter — two lovely black-haired beauties, Adriana, eight years in age, and the other, Natalia, seven. While I was watching them tease their young cousin, the listless bean-snipper, Despina excused herself and went over to reprimand them.

~ ~ ~ ~ ~ ~ ~

The sun was now beginning to set, casting a great orange shroud upon Mesta. Pretty quickly, Despina returned, with an oval-shaped porcelain platter mounted high with my first meal on this island: grilled zucchini, fried eggplant, cut tomatoes, fresh yoghurt, homemade feta cheese, dried Kalamata olives, a little pitcher of olive oil, and wonderful crusty dark bread. Where did all this good food come from, I wondered in silence.

The food was eaten with relish, some of it shared with Despina. The sun went down, and the glow of the evening cast a magic spell upon the village inhabitants, who were now oozing out of all doors and dark alleyways, little by little, and filtering into the square. I was thoroughly amused. Dmitri had told me that this village square is the grand central place of all activities: celebrational, political, jovial, analytical, intractable, unmanageable, unresolvable, and the variations went on. Despina assured me I would be there long enough to observe, perhaps even participate in, a number of those, particularly if she had anything to do with initiating them.

For now, on this first full day, feeling a little weary and exhausted, I decided to leave the revelers to their convivial escapades, and head for my white-washed room behind the blue door. I couldn't guarantee it would be for the night, but at least for a late evening nap.

~ ~ ~ ~ ~ ~ ~

Turns out I did sleep through that first night, but I was pleasantly awakened at earliest dawn by the sounds of three church bells announcing Sunday morning in varying cadences. I thought a meander back to the square would be interesting and found the place desolate and completely my own. The village was still fast asleep and no one stirred. In one corner, the cobble sweeper, crumpled and slumbering on his stool, clutching his twiggy broom, and in another corner, the gatekeeper sitting on a rock next to one of the village entrances, clutching his ring of keys and sleeping as if night was going to continue all day.

~ ~ ~ ~ ~ ~ ~

In the utter stillness of this morning, in a solitary space, I wrote in my journal:

I am experiencing a wonderful sense of balance as I extract from within me all the best reasons to be alive. Mesta is intoxicating me with a renewed life. I hear foghorns in tandem on the sea as the morning mist evaporates. I see window shutters all around the square still closed. Nothing is moving. Above me, the village church's tower points to a blue and cloudless sky.

~ ~ ~ ~ ~ ~ ~

I was not quite finished writing, when Despina showed up, barely awake but eager for her cup of double espresso.

I was curious to hear more of Despina's story, and she continued: "I was born and raised in Mesta," she said. "At the age of eighteen, I wandered to America, to the city of Queens in New York State, where I stayed for several years mostly to learn English. I also had my two children in Queens." She told me she did not know who the fathers were but that that was not particularly important to her. Just about then, two village elders, one of them carrying his narghile, sat down on her side of the square, and she needed to attend to them. "They are regulars," she said, and then added with a smile, "and they are on my side!" Little by little, the villagers began gathering for their Sunday morning coffee conversations, and soon both taverns were about one-third full. Interesting to me was that Despina's tavern drew mostly younger people, and most of the elderly gathered at Stavros' tavern.

Observing Despina serve her clientele, I was amused. Contrary to tradition, especially for women with children, and much to the shameful chagrin of older women in the village, she defiantly wore shorts and tank tops while serving tables, even on Sunday, and was, in general, the epitome of a thoroughly modern Millie, finished off with plenty of attitude — certainly not a representative of customs and rituals of ancient Greece. At the ripe old age of twenty-six, it was her mission, she told me, to upgrade the level of equality among the ladies and men of the village, but most of all, to prove to the men that women were equally important in life, that they were equally strong, not to mention equally capable of running any public organization, be it for business, pleasure, or politics.

She finished serving everyone and came back to my table.

"Stavros, on the 'other' side of the square, is one such macho Greek," she confided. "He hates the ground I stand on." I had watched him long enough to see he was doing everything in his power to chide and berate Despina, by talking to his guests about her, maliciously and in half-whispers, convincing them she was a woman of ill repute. A shameful woman should not be running a business while leaving her children to scuttle and scamper about, he had once said to one of her own acquaintances.

To add even more venom to his extreme dislike for her, he began telling everyone that she was also living unlawfully with a man, Giannis, her partner in the business.

Obviously Despina was a complete no-no for the old Greek guard, but undaunted and fearless, she remained steadfast in her battle against the outdated customs of what she considered a very undignified Greek male society, of which Stavros, in her opinion, was the prime leader, by example. By considering herself the perfect emissary for younger Greek women, she was fighting for liberation from old-fashioned principles and concepts, including standards of public affectionate behavior between men and women. She was not to be antagonized at any cost; Despina could rage! And few there would be with defenses sturdy enough to withstand such a barrage of verbal artillery in concentrated discharge. She was The Scarlet Lady of Mesta, I thought with a smile.

Just then, within the evident disparity among a few of the villagers, alarm in the midst of this peaceful ambience was set off when Despina, according to Stavros, had walked too closely past his tavern and upset the mood of his clientele. The spell of calm was suddenly broken when he began throwing loud verbal accusations at her from his side of the square. I stayed where I was, on the periphery, and watched, and rationalized that where there are more than two gathered in the name of an entangled universe, interpretations of opinions and understanding will clash. And so it was in Mesta, in this nearly-thousand-year-old tiny covered fortress. The old fight, for the oldest reason, in this old world, was still going on. Who was right and who was wrong? And each would hold to his own forever.

~ ~ ~ ~ ~ ~ ~

The word 'mesta', in the Greek language, means 'hard,' as in opposite of 'tender.' I was watching the real meaning of tenderlessness evolve during that week, as tensions mounted and restlessness grew. Not only was it an inner village war of sexes, wills, and genders that was festering; it quickly exploded into an even bigger matter, regarding the location of the two taverns on this square, and their accessibility to visitors to the fortress from neighboring villages.

It was agreed, therefore, that on a certain morning several village fathers and state policemen in uniform were to show up, to measure the square and write reports, to hopefully settle the dispute . . . and then, Despina devilishly pointed out: ". . . they will all hang around later for free ouzo! I have plenty of it on the shelf, so I will win this little battle." Such a pack of dynamite, that girl, with an uncanny ability to crush even the policeman's ego. She was out to conquer, and she was completely convinced that Stavros would live to regret he had ever tried to banter and chaff with her. The contest was on. In her own pugnacious way, she would win this war, and not without laying cost on her contender.

~ ~ ~ ~ ~ ~ ~

Things calmed down somewhat, and I went to sit back down in Despina's tavern. I wrote in my journal:

Whatever the outcome will be in this little dispute, in this ancient place, slow and quiet within its venerable walls, Mesta is simply this place, a live piece of history, living. It is a reminder that the distinction between heaven and earth is the same everywhere. Everywhere has a little of both, in many shapes, colors, and sizes.

Here in Mesta, heaven means sitting on the platias surrounded by huge stone pillars and thick stone walls, where mornings arrive as bright as tropical sun, and evenings fall as softly as fruit from a tree.

Earth means every villager is vitally involved in the wellbeing of his own little patch. There is Dmitri, who oversees this responsibility in large part as he continues his own interest in the history and preservation of Mesta, from its pre-Hellenic times to the present, from historical Arab pirate raids through Justinian, Byzantine, Genoan, and Turkish occupations.

It is evening time in Mesta. The rebels have left the battlefield, as the sun sets on another day of events, both frivolous and rebellious. Soon the gatekeeper will wend his way to the West gate, to lock it for the night, but not before I zig-zag once more, quickly, through the passages to the West portal just ahead of him, to step out to the edge, and sigh. The sea is smooth and violet, with streaks of turquoise blue, glistening in patches outlined by fine lines of silver. I feel as if any moment Chios will rise out of the sea and float away to infinity.

~ ~ ~ ~ ~ ~ ~

And then morning comes again. Slowly the village awakens once more, its sounds and activities begin to unfold like a fugue-ish symphony. The cobble sweeper comes through with his twig broom to sweep yesterday out of existence. The gatekeeper has already unlocked the gates and is back on his other stony bollard, in front of the village priest's domicile, never losing his grip on that ring of keys. As I walk by him toward the tavern for my morning espresso, he throws the biggest smile. The square's fountain gurgles away, and sparrows fly in for their daily bath. Blankets, quilts, and eiderdown pillows, are being aired out on window ledges. I reach the tavern just as Despina is watering the geraniums in the hanging pots. She winks and I know she's got the espresso machine prepped in her kitchen.

While watching this little square come to life on this morning, the fishmonger comes through with seven fish on the rope at the end of his pole, freshly caught at sunrise this morning. "Fresh fish, come get your fresh fish," he intones in a chant of his own linguistic composition and cadence. Instantly, kitchen shutters fly open in ascending scale patterns. Buxom housewives with aprons have heard his cry, and they yell out of their ground floor windows, "Save one for me, please!" Across the square, another echoes the same. And a gentleman, sitting in his usual morning spot near the tavern entrance, has asked Despina: "When does the fruit wagon come again?"

"Tomorrow," she responds, as she sits down to join me for our morning java ritual.

"So, Despina, who won the battle yesterday?" I ask, with some cynicism.

She gives me one of her wily smiles: "No one did, but it was fun! And anyway, I don't care. I have decided I want to leave this crazy place and go back to Queens with my daughters."

~ ~ ~ ~ ~ ~ ~

Gradually, everything gets into full swing for the day. An old wooden door creaks on its hinges as the village storekeeper opens shop. I walk by to see what she's selling. Despina explained to me she is the proprietress of all village conveniences, as needed. In her little space, she runs a post office and a drugstore, besides selling small souvenirs to the few tourists who venture through. "Yesterday," Despina told me, "she had a good day. She sold some camera film for three drachmas. And, oh," she said with a mischievous twinkle in her eye, "I bought a postage stamp." I looked at her with some curiosity. "Yes, for a letter to Queens!"

I grinned from ear to ear, knowing Despina had surely been up to her tricks. I went over to buy a few postcards, and on the way out of the shop to go home, I leaned down to stroke the tummy of Calypso, the only domesticated cat in the village, stretched out on a stone tile in the warmth of the sun.

~ ~ ~ ~ ~ ~ ~

Once again in my journal:

In this little world, villagers gather every day over coffee, wine, or beer, to hear news from the other end of the fortress or from the other side of the square, and to carry on with their daily rituals and customs.

From the stoop in front of my vaulted home, I enjoy my neighbor lady whisking by with a fried fish still sizzling in her pan. She's heading to her friend, next door, to give her a taste, reaching through the window to do so. Excitement mounts with each bite while they discuss their repast with animation and finger-licking enthusiasm, making sure not to miss a single oily crumb, and emitting toothless smiles as though they have a big secret. It is an image I have difficulty discarding at the end of the day.

~ ~ ~ ~ ~ ~ ~

All in all, the days were rolling by much too quickly, but the charm of this island was destined to stay with me into posterity. In front of my door in the middle of my stay, I spotted a most beautiful iridescent scarab beetle, about an inch and one-half long, glowing in a lustrous display of luminous blue-green intensity. Evidently, his karma was ailing slightly; he seemed to be ill. I was thrilled. This was a very significant compliment to me. Throughout ancient folklore, the scarab has been the single most revered beetle in every way. He brings good luck and fortune. A scarab is a talisman of the soul, a very powerful omen possessing supernatural and magical elements.

Poor little fellow succumbed during the following night, much to my joy, because I had decided I would love to try to smuggle him home to San Francisco as my own talisman. There were no ants about, so I placed him on a rock protrusion outside my door, to let him dry up for a few days before wrapping him in soft toilet tissue, and putting him inside a wide-capped aspirin bottle, in which he could travel safely. I'm happy to report, little Aristotle made it all through Turkey on the next leg of my travels and eventually home to California. Not even the Turkish customs officer discovered, or smelled, him. This little guy really stank, in fact; proof, I suppose, that he was definitely hatched in a dung heap somewhere.

~ ~ ~ ~ ~ ~ ~

On my last evening in Mesta, on this rugged island of Chios, I took a drive at dusk, a few kilometers along the edge of the island to a beautiful little harbor at Emporius, which Dmitri had told me about. It was not very far away. I found a table among a few other revelers at its seaside café, ordered a glass of chilled retsina, and let the tranquility of the night and the moment infuse me. Behind the only sailboat anchored in this tiny harbor, a full moon was rising. I watched it grow from big and round and orange on the horizon, to a sleek and silver orb perched high in the sky. This night was a perfect pause inside the majesty and silence of Greek antiquity. Before leaving, I wandered down to the water's edge, to touch the by-now inky-colored sea and decided life need be no bigger than that.

~ ~ ~ ~ ~ ~ ~

It had become obvious to me at the end of my stay in Mesta that leaving it would be sad. For me, it had represented all the sensual and intellectual pleasures of Greece. But the time had come. Dmitri knocked on my door to help me with my bag, and together we strolled back across that notorious square once more. The gatekeeper got off his rock to finally seize the moment and wrap his long gangly arms around me for an uncustomary hug. Dmitri's wife, Purla, was waiting in the doorway of their dwelling for her turn with a rigorous handshake. Then she handed me a bag full of pine nuts, and some figs wrapped in sackcloth. And little but mighty Despina, weeping by her kitchen stove, came over to say goodbye with a smile through big crocodile tears, before she handed over a little jar of preserved limes.

Such a fiesta!

Such a memory!

Mesta, a sleepy Greek sabbatical.

Efharisto!! Thank you!

CROSSING THE PLAINS

My dear Dad had passed away of old age in July. He had lived a long and fulfilled life. I flew back to his home in Winnipeg, Manitoba in November, to sort through books, boxes, and bits of memorabilia, to go through all of Dad's doodles and diaries of dramas and dreams, all of which I would then load into a rental car, drive away from the Canadian outback for the last time, and head to my home in San Francisco. It was my wonderful eleven-day solitary road trip, beginning in North Dakota, and across some of America's most awe-inspiring and expansive country, the great Northwest. A liberating and magical journey, to say the least. I came through it unscathed, without a scratch, encountering no physical or mechanical problems whatsoever, and apparently managing to travel the roads well ahead of inclement Winter weather systems.

Setting out on an early morning, I could feel my rhythms lining up. Large lazy crystal snowflakes were falling at midday, giving me only momentary cause for worry, because I was too jazzed about the journey to think about Winter obstacles, any obstacles for that matter. I was eager to move ahead in the full knowledge that I would make it, one day at a time, one mile at a time, one moment at a time. I was remembering Luis Bunuel's words that allude to having courage to leave one's destiny to chance and going with the fundamental mystery on the metaphoric roads ahead. An infinite expectation of the daily dawn was all the assurance I needed – on any day. Each mile that disappeared through the rear-view mirror would be a mile I would never again see, in this chapter. No way to hang on to them. Besides, this journey had no agendas, no mapped-out road plans, no itineraries. I was simply traveling toward completion of another episode of my life, malleable to the idea of letting every day offer what it wanted to.

And so I drove, westward along the endless superhighways of America, with the whole countryside to myself all day, and very few cars or big-rigs going or coming. I sat back and enjoyed the Great Plains roll by. North Dakota! The name itself evoked so many images of a vast land, a founding people, and a particular style of life: the American West, the Native American, the Frontier, stark beauty, sameness of an unforgiving land, pioneer spirits, independence, hard work, and lives of adventure, freedom, and opportunity.

Being alone, seeing all this quietly by myself, evoked tremendous mystical feelings, and filled me with so much joy, it became necessary now and then to get out of the car on the side of the road, and just shout out to three hundred and sixty degrees of protective horizon.

Pushing along the winding Missouri River was exquisitely magnificent, providing a promise of solace and consolation. I wondered about the relationship between the people and the land. Depending upon one's point of view, the land could be life-giving or life-threatening. I was familiar with all of that, having lived on the central Canadian prairies, where the reality of the land was not always heartwarming. I suspected this landscape had changed little since the first impressions were ever documented. It seemed to be a land where time stopped still several millenniums ago and not much changed, ever after.

At the end of a day, and still in North Dakota, I began to feel how my mind had been metaphorically opened and widened, a perfect receptacle for good thoughts. Amazing thing, that human mind!

I checked into a drive-by motel at a place the map called Beulah, and headed for the bar and lounge. Fresh out of organic Northern California, I found myself in the smokiest lounge I had ever been in and wondered if North Dakota was even part of this wide union of states. But what was I thinking? It was Monday night football across America, at least across this America. This . . . North Dakota! And men smoked and drank beer in these sports bars.

If it wasn't much else, it was definitely my first introduction to a different attitude about lounges and bars. No romantic little round cocktail tables here, with wrought iron chairs and people having quiet, stare-in-your-eye, philosophical dialogue, or listening to mandolin strums and accordion sighs coming from musicians in the bar's corner. This was a true man's drinking bar, a Western man at that, with long tables off to the side for wives and kids. Lots of noise and raucous laughter, beer puddles on the floor, and about five large television screens hanging around the entire room, all of them resonating with the great American football ritual. The bar counter itself was obviously for the odd ones in, the out-of-towners, the . . . misfits! Since I qualified for each category, I stepped up, plopped myself on a bar stool, with two empties next to me. This made me smile, wondering who would dare to sit there at some point this evening! I ordered the usual glass of red and paid the bartender . . . wait! Two dollars and fifty cents? Impossible! And the glass!? They only had beer-drinking-sized glasses, so I got a beer glass, half filled with their version of red wine. "Cheers!" I said, and swiveled around to watch the people.

Within minutes, a very handsome cowboy came up. "Mind if I sit next to you, ma'am?"

"Not at all, make yourself comfortable!" I said, noticing his tall stature, his greasy leather cowboy hat, his beautifully aged leather jacket, leather chaps, through which I could see holes in the butt of his jeans when he stood up to get change out of his pocket, and a pair of very handsome I would say handmade Argentinian cowboy boots with spurs. Wow! The complete package!

"You're visiting, are you, ma'am?" he inquired. I smiled; didn't take him long to figure that out.

"Yes," I said, "I'm on a road trip across North Dakota, through the Northwest, and on down to San Francisco." He was mightily impressed.

"Alone?" he wanted to know.

"Yes, alone. My father passed away recently, and I'm hauling back a few boxes of memorabilia from his home in central Canada."

I wondered then what may have crossed his mind at hearing the word 'alone'. I turned to him and asked the obvious rhetorical question: "You're a cowboy from the looks of it?!"

"Yes ma'am, I own two thousand acres o' land and several hundred horses near Beulah, just down the road; I have five children, nineteen grandchildren, and . . . " he paused, " . . . no wife!"

And then he gave me the obvious look. Except I couldn't quite tell if he was just plain sad or looking for a hopeful pickup. I jumped ahead of him by saying, playfully, mind you, "Sir, I am not interested in 'coming up to see your etchings'!" making the quote signs in the air with my fingers!

That threw him for a moment, and he replied: "Uh, ma'am, I don't rightly know what you mean by that, but I was intendin' to ask if you might have time to come over and see ma beautiful horses 'fore you leave!"

"You know, there's a real cutie at the other end of this bar who might well be interested in your offer . . . . Why don't you give her a try?" I suggested. He was a bit disappointed, and took a moment to recover.

"But she's young and you're wise." he came back.

I thanked him for the compliment and then, to try to change the subject, I asked him: "What age are you then?"

"I'm about your age, fifty-six!" Whereupon I laughed out loud and grabbed his arm (felt that amazingly soft leather jacket), and thanked him again. I really needed to get a bite to eat, and then catch my sleep for the next day's adventure.

He got off his stool when I did, and reaching for my hand to kiss it, he looked up at me, saying: "Happy trails, ma'am. Nice knowin' ya!" I left, and just before I disappeared through the door, I turned back to take a look. He was tilting his hat toward me, like a good cowboy would.

~ ~ ~ ~ ~ ~ ~

A highly-diluted cup of good old motel-perked coffee-no-cream got me started in the morning. A gas fill-up, a bag of roasted cashews, and I was good for the next hundred miles. It took only a few minutes to get out of Beulah, and already I could see fields of cattle grazing, ranchland extending to the horizon, and the landscape 'decorated' here and there with rusty old broken-down stoves and one or two once-stylish Chevys, soon to be at the fierce mercy of Winter's wrath.

About thirty miles into the journey, a sign said 'Medora -- Teddy Roosevelt's Other Home'. Regardless of any decision I might have made to stop or not, the forces of nature obligated me to pull over and get out of the car. An unbounded view and breathtaking landscape immediately enveloped me. Absolute stillness in surround sound! The only actual sounds I heard were a lone crow and the swish of the wind whistling across small canyons. I had reached the eastern edge of The Badlands, an area of the Dakotas known for its scenic and rugged terrain, a mysterious place on Earth which the Native Americans refer to as 'the land God forgot'. I was filled with awe as I glanced all around me at the magnificence of this naked mass of land.

I drove into Medora, and conveniently, at the end of its only street, the Cowboy Café drew me in for a hopeful cup of desperately needed 'real' coffee. Two women, one of them calling herself the local historian, owned and ran the place, a perfect relic describing bygone times and activities; walls randomly plastered with brown-edged sepia photographs of past eras; wall-shelves littered with a hundred empty tin cans, labeled for coffee beans, lentils, cornstarch, baking soda, grits, hominy, and the like; and thick wooden benches and tables carved up with symbols indicating the many cattle brands in the area.

Greeted with a very open and friendly good morning, I asked for that cup of coffee, and the other one retorted with a resounding "Yes, ma'am, and a real cup it will be, too!" It was. Some chat about local folklore and Teddy Roosevelt's log cabin, visible just up the road, and my mug was empty. I sauntered out the door and side-stepped briefly into what was once a motel, now a bookstore, filled with old and new books, and, much to my elation and surprise, a series of purchasable CDs of probably every collection of cowboy songs known to man. I was thrilled to find one that included all and more of the cowboy songs Dad used to sing for us during frozen Winter evenings on the Manitoba prairie, self-accompanied by his hand-made guitar and a harmonica. Paying for my goods at the cash register, a genuine old-fashioned brass construct with a big pull-down lever, I fell into conversation with the proprietress, who seemed a little starved for chat. In a lone minute, she told me how she and her writer husband had recently turned this place, once their motel business, into the current bookstore, and we talked about taking risks, being courageous, and the discipline of bettering our lives.

"Thank you for stopping by," she said with a proud tone in her voice, "in our little forgotten part of the world, in this small corner of North Dakota, the state few know about."

I decided right then to tell her my story, indirectly about North Dakota, more directly about Grand Forks. "I had been researching prices and possibilities for the car rental several months ago, in preparation for this journey from Grand Forks to San Francisco," I told her. "I rang up one of the better known rental agencies, and they gave me some outrageous estimate I was unwilling to commit to! My first suspicion was the person on the phone did not know his geography very well. So, I asked him if he knew where Grand Forks was. He did not know. And finally I wanted to know, 'Where am I speaking to, what city are you in?'

"'I'm in Missouri, ma'am', he grumbled at me with plenty of disdain. 'Are you a teacher or something!'

"'No, I'm not a teacher,' I told him, 'but I'm a traveler, and I am from Canada. While I take for granted that not many people are familiar with the geography of Canada, you, sir, aren't exactly familiar with the geography of your own country! But thank you for your information and time. Goodbye.'"

The proprietress of the bookstore was enjoying the tale. And I continued: "I rang another one-eight-hundred number for car rentals. This time an English-speaking though foreign voice answered: 'Good morning, ma'am. How may I help you?'

"'Could you give me an estimate for a car rental for one week, pick-up in Grand Forks and drop-off in San Francisco?'

"'I know where San Francisco is, but I have no idea where Grand Forks is,' she said, in an embarrassed tone of voice. 'I am from the Philippines, where I am right now, but I lived in Oregon for a few years, and I think Grand Forks is on the West Coast somewhere, yes?'

"'No, Grand Forks is in North Dakota, in the middle North of the United States, near the Canadian border.' I waited for her estimate and said thank you; it, too, was much too high, and based, I assumed pompously, on ignorance of both facts and geography."

By now, the lady proprietress was laughing out loud. "How did this search end?" she was eager to know.

"I rang one more one-eight-hundred number for car rental information. 'Hello madam, how may I help you?' a male voice said, in an unmistakable Eastern Indian accent. And I noticed he said 'madam', including the 'd' in the middle.

"I asked him the same question. I could hear a computer keyboard tapping sound, and quickly he gave me a very satisfying estimate, less than half compared to what the others had offered. I was so happily surprised, I immediately asked for a confirmation number so this reservation could be permanently plugged in. He was very polite, very efficient, effusively thankful, and then of course I had to ask: 'What part of the world am I calling this time?'

"'You are speaking to Calcutta, India, madam!' he said. I was charmed by the way he added 'India', but, being the cynic that I am, I supposed there was the possibility that some person might think Calcutta was in Africa!

"'And you apparently know where Grand Forks is?' I was dying to know for sure.

"'Yes, of course, madam, it is in North Dakota!' he said, full of confidence and complete conviction.

"'But you live so far away, sir,' I retorted, quite dumbfounded, but ever so pleased.

"'Yes,' he said, 'but that's no excuse not to know where the world cities are. It's part of my job . . . and we have Google,' he added with a giggle. I was imminently relieved someone from so far away not only knew where Grand Forks was but called it a 'world city.'

"There you have the story . . . !" I said.

The proprietress beamed from ear to ear. "You have made my day," she said, so thankfully. "I think I will stay in Medora a few more years!"

I danced back out to my sexy little car, revved up the motor, threw the CD with the cowboy songs into the player, and took off along the highway westward. In seconds, I was levitating. The music was spot-on for The Badlands. And Dad? He was right there, yodeling and whistling and strumming his guitar and singing along next to me in the rider's seat. My car seemed to be fueled with extra zest on this beautiful morning. And I was full of enthusiasm for a wondrous ride through the rugged terrain of deep canyons and jagged buttes created by millions of years of wind, water, and erosion. A vast area of earthly riches with exotic rock masses poking into view all the way along a lunar look-alike landscape. Way off in the distance, right in the middle of a giant horizon, I spotted a lone log cabin while here in the comfortable interior of my little car, and the CD just happened to be playing 'Home on the Range.' The uplift was magical, and I felt I had, at long last, become the master and commander of my journey, of my life, of my days ahead. Each mile disappearing behind me was mine to remember and treasure forever. My spirits were dancing across these great Plains of the Dakotas. Now and then, a black cloud of Canada geese moved across the sky, heading South for the Winter.

From the map, I was sad to see I would soon be leaving North Dakota, but I would never forget it. The day had its noteworthy moment however, ending in a small historical town named Livingston, on the border of North Dakota and Montana. Driving down its main boulevard, I felt a little as if I had landed on a wintery movie set from the Wild West days. I parked the car against a slippery iced-over curb. At the street corner, while trying to cross, an old trucker stopped in the middle of the intersection, motioning for me to go ahead, then rolled down his window, and yelled out: "Something wrong if a guy can't let a young girl cross the street!" In a boutique-y coffee house, its windows all steamed up from the warmth of fresh pastry smells and espresso machines hissing with each emission, I took a chance and ordered an au lait. The young guy behind the counter, not surprisingly, knew exactly what I meant. The place was teeming with youthful activity, university students engaged in debate and discussion, new-age bohemians reading French literature (I noticed Camus on one cover), and hitch-hiking travelers just arriving from nearby Yellowstone Park, I heard them say, coming in to sit by the open fireplace.

I took a sip of coffee, looked around, and remembered a book I had read called 'Road Fever,' by Tim Cahill, another favorite travel writer, who lives here in Livingston. It was the unbelievable story of his Guinness world record road trip from Patagonia to North Alaska. I wished, silently, I'd had it with me right now. Never know if he might just walk in for a cup of steaming espresso . . .

TINY PAINTED PAPER BAGS

Many inspirational bits and evocative pieces of wisdom have, over the years, been stuck to the wall of my study. There's one in particular that feels like a great way to begin this story. It is from an author of motivational writings, Mary Anne Radmacher, and in part reads: "Live with intention. Walk to the edge. Play with abandon. Choose with no regret. Continue to learn." It was not by chance that these words formed the composite that accompanied me on an unprecedented journey into the laboratory of evolution in the Archipelago of the Galapagos Islands.

As a young teenager during the Fifties, I had become fascinated reading, at my father's urging, the Life Magazine story about a third-generation Belgian family surnamed de Roy, who had, a few years prior, decided to close their doors in Bruxelles, leave behind centuries of culture and civilization, and sail bravely and specifically toward the relatively unknown and unexplored Galapagos islands. Their first-born daughter, Tui, already two, was with them; a son named Jean was born later on the islands.

Tui essentially grew up a native of the Galapagos. With her father's help, including the building of various boats for her expeditions, she was not only encouraged, but inspired to explore and discover her new world. With firsthand knowledge, deeply spiritual awareness, and respectful enthusiasm, she spent her entire life inhaling the history and natural processes of the Galapagos islands.

Long before embarking upon my own journey to this Archipelago, I had now and then been poring through the pages of one of Tui's narrated photography collections which I had on my bookshelf, and I became spellbound by her ability to capture the essence of the Galapagos in word and photo image. "These islands have remained in a time capsule," she wrote, "a small sample of prehistoric days cast adrift through the ages."

It was this same book that at the end of my stay in the Galapagos ultimately provided the reason for one fugitive moment in this great web of life — a situation of separation by one degree, if you will.

~ ~ ~ ~ ~ ~ ~ ~

A visually inspiring flight to Ecuador lined my heart with all the right colors and moods, and armed me with all the exhilaration needed for an unusual adventure. Awestruck, I stared out of the airplane window at the sea of brilliant orange and luminous pink flat cloud variations, some looking like floating mashed-potato clumps outlined in red and gold, all lined up against the sun setting fiery red into the horizon somewhere over the Caribbean.

The night-time landing in Quito, no less breathtaking, was like flying into a giant stone-carved fruit bowl filled to the brim with sparkling jewels, an ambient city spread out like a yellow diamond necklace on mounds of black velvet inside the abruptly protruding Andean massif nine-thousand feet above the Pacific Ocean.

Flying six hundred miles westward the following morning toward the Galapagos proved equally inspiring.

Beginning the descent, I could see the cluster of islands, looking like monstrous brown dragons floating in one gigantic pile in the big blue Pacific. I also sensed a place where the bountiful sea had rumbled and roared for millenniums while these islands slumbered.

Once on terra firma, I could feel I was in a place where earth seemed utterly untamed; where moods could no doubt range easily and suddenly from serene and somber to nerve-tingling natural violence. Here was a paradise, neither found nor lost, neither harried nor hurried, and at peace with time. What manifested itself immediately was that this little Archipelago was not a holiday resort!

As the days proceeded, guided expeditions revealed everything from the islands' innermost natural activities to nature's outermost natural evolutions, and I was reminded that, in this secluded environment for the undisturbed expansion of indigenous species, on land, in the air, and in the sea, I was very much a second-class citizen.

On land: ancient turtles, ambling; entwined iguanas, motionless; black lizards, camouflaged; flightless cormorants, lumbering; blue-footed boobies, courting; red-throated frigates, mating; and yellow-billed albatrosses, strutting.

In the air: oystercatchers plunging into the sea for dinner; swallow-tailed gulls in lofty flight patterns; pink flamingos soaring; storm petrels jostling for cliff space; pelicans swooping; hawks gawking; plovers dancing; and yes, those tiny Darwin finches all vying for landing patches on yellow prickly pear blossoms.

In the near sea: wobbly penguins gliding with ease through the watery brink; orange ceramic-looking crabs cavorting on backs of sleeping sea lions.

And in the farther deep: giant manta rays, sharks, dolphins, star fish, and millions upon millions of fish species, each inhabiting their territorial space in a deep, blue-green watery kingdom.

~ ~ ~ ~ ~ ~ ~

Having spent this last day strolling through shrubbery forests in search of ancient land turtles, and walking through endless arterial lava tunnels, we were asked to regroup and meet our rattly old bus near the little stands where villagers were selling homemade banana juice. Nearby, I noticed another rustic little stand, on one side selling crudely strung necklaces of local rock chips and, off to the other side, a curiously tiny huddle of flat brown paper baggies, each with an originally painted island scene.

I loved them immediately!

While pondering whether to purchase the entire lot, a young girl appeared. Guessing her to be twelve years of age, I was instantly struck by her olive-colored, translucent face, perfectly framed by a glowing mop of tangled straw-blond hair. Her brown almond-shaped eyes reflected purest joy.

My glance, alternating between the innocent beauty radiating from her and the colorful pile of brown paper baggies, was suddenly interrupted when she saw me looking at them.

"Do you like them?" she burst forth with all her enthusiasm intact. I realized instantly she spoke perfect, rather aristocratic, English.

"It's my artwork, I painted them all, and I have more!" she offered. I was completely captivated, by her charm, her brilliance, and her intelligence. But I was also puzzled as to who she was. She didn't seem to be pure Ecuadoran.

"You are a very fine artist," I told her, and then dared to ask if I might purchase the lot of the baggies, sixteen in all. She beamed, and pranced all the way around to the front of the table, next to me, and handed them to me personally.

"And the price?" I asked.

Without hesitation, and with complete self-confidence, she responded: "Twenty-five cents each."

While pulling out a few one dollar bills for her, I dared to inquire:

"Who are you, young lady, and where are you from? I'm curious about you — your curly brown-blonde hair, and your perfect English."

She smiled broadly, and pointing to the backside of one of the baggies — where I hadn't thought to look — she said: "That's me! I'm Natalie de Roy!"

My heart stopped.

"Natalie, so nice to meet you. Are you by chance . . . ?" and before I could finish, she responded almost automatically, having probably been asked the same question before.

"Yes, I am the daughter of Jean de Roy, Tui is my aunt! And this," pointing to the petite woman across the table, "is my mother, Marie, who is half Ecuadoran and half Chinese!"

The marked physical contrast between the two — Marie dressed in black laces and bangles, with very long, very black, very straight hair — made it all the more interesting and, of course, explained Natalie's exotic mix.

Feeling quite speechless, I shook Natalie's hand, while she smiled up at me. "It is so special to meet you," I said. "I know the story about your grandparents' odyssey to these islands fifty-some years ago; and here you are, now the third generation of de Roys in the Galapagos." Natalie, nodding acknowledgment, just kept smiling and didn't say another word.

"I wish you well, and please paint some more baggies! They are beautiful," I told her, reluctant to leave.

Sauntering back to the waiting bus, I turned around a few times and saw Natalie waving. She kept waving, until I could see her no longer.

In my hand, more or less piled this way and that, were sixteen tiny precious brown paper baggies, each one painted with glowing original watercolors, each one depicting a different Galapagos mood, but collectively — and through the innocent eyes of Natalie — holding a most unique treasury of memories for me. One was still turned backwards, and I saw it again: her own young signature, Natalie de Roy, the goldenest little thread in this strange Belgian/Galapagos tapestry, proof that within the circle of synchronicity, there are no accidents.

Natalie was meant to happen for me.

ANYA OF HELSINKI

ST. PETERSBURG, RUSSIA
September 2003

After several dispirited days and gloomy nights in a dank, oppressive apartment, with bathroom floods and non-functioning heaters, not to mention a crumbling and dangerous mess of concrete with protruding rusty nails and bits of pointed metal right outside the apartment door, I woke up one morning with an intense urge to leave Haymarket Square for a day. Historical and famous, or not, its debilitated surroundings and decrepit buildings were not inspiring. I gathered up all my writing materials, my postcards, and my journal, and headed over to the comfortable, warm, dry, sunny hotel café of the century-old Hotel Astoria, just a few blocks away.

Entering the palatial foyer of the hotel, I was escorted by a uniformed concierge with a somewhat stiff demeanor to a cheerful corner of the hotel's opulent loggia. There was the perfectly comfortable seat near a tall window with the warm sun streaming in. I unloaded all my accessories, and stared out of that big window for a minute. To the left, St. Isaac's Cathedral, with one of the largest and overbearing domes I had ever seen, outside of St. Peter's in Rome; and to the right, within easy walking distance, the venerable old Hermitage, some of whose many rooms filled with historical artwork I had already visited several times. An inspiring view for this afternoon's journalizing, I thought, and the perfect antithesis to my daily distressed environment in the neglected and shabby Haymarket.

I felt no dejection whatsoever as I sank myself into a puffy sage-green brocaded settee, enhanced by a black marble-top coffee table before me. How nice it would be, I thought, to indulge in a four-star afternoon by starting off with a chocolate espresso. In St. Petersburg, that's an espresso with a piece of dark chocolate on the side. Eventually, my plan was to follow that with a glass of bordeaux, a choice I had noticed on their very sophisticated wine list, and, interspersed with postcards I wanted to write, simply while away the afternoon watching a very colorful coterie of sophisticated world travelers traverse this grand and opulent foyer.

My steaming hot espresso arrived, impeccably served in a gold-rimmed black porcelain mini-cup set on a gold-rimmed black porcelain saucer, with three bits of dark chocolate in a little gold-rimmed black porcelain plate on the side. A shiny silver pitcher of ice water completed the service with perfect old world elegance. I was captivated by the demure young hostess, costumed in her heavily starched blue uniform and white bonnet, her effortlessness and smoothness of manner infinitely refined.

I sat back and took a deep breath, feeling exuberant and in high spirits. Happily settled and well-placed, I wanted to drift into a dream, as I slumped into the bottom of this lusciously cushioned surrounding — a tiny bit of clean and fluffy heaven in gritty old St. Petersburg. How uplifting to take a break from chipped coffee mugs, four-legged stools with one leg missing, and a half-painted wooden table, which, albeit, did have its charm when in my ardent imagination I envisioned Dostoyevsky sitting right there, creating some of the most important literary works known to scholars.

But to the task at hand: I organized my postcards in one pile, address book next to that. Then came seventeen colorful stamps carefully displayed and admired for a moment, remembering how, the previous day, I had put out a valiant effort to find them in three different post offices; a labor of love, indeed, but given my passion for sending postcards from faraway places to friends across the planet, it was all part of the adventure. Pleased and smiling broadly, I placed my wire-rimmed spectacles on my nose and finally began my writing project. One sip of this Russian espresso concoction bolted me into action and the first postcard was written and addressed to Dad, of course.

The second postcard would have been addressed to my mother. It was in that moment I felt just a little sad that she was no longer around for me to tell her I finally made it to Russia, the place she dreaded and disliked so much due to atrocious experiences remembered from her childhood. I would have written: "Dearest Mother, I am, at long last, in your country of birth, and here to tell you it is, after the many years since your departure, truly a well-lit and wonderful place. You would have been proud to walk hand in hand with me along the main boulevard, Ñevsky Prospect, with its many fur hat shops and cobblers still crafting boots for hundreds of men and women, like your father did. Here and there, you would have recognized a poor peasant woman on a corner selling her three loaves of homemade bread, a scene that would have elicited tears from your eyes and brought back a hundred memories from long ago."

Shaking myself free of my reverie of the moment, I was about to begin writing the next postcard, when a retinue of rather raucous people caught my attention in the foyer behind me. An elderly-looking personage had arrived, followed by a mini-entourage of servants: a driver, a personal attendant carrying two of her three bags, and another carrying a third.

I would describe her as a rather overbearing Victorian madame who, with her embarrassingly capacious paunch, wandered about as if she owned the entire first floor. Her left hand flailed about in perfect rhythm to a stream of rude reprimands in Russian directed at her obedient attendants, while her right hand waved her walking stick to emphasize the beat. The spectacle was not unlike an ancient comedic troupe performing in the lobby for the entertainment of visitors. My solitude was of course completely shattered and interrupted, but my curiosity was quickly and fully absorbed.

Madame's antics didn't end there. Shuffling madly past me and just ahead to the next window seat, she was unsuccessful in trying to coax the very young couple sitting across from one another one table over into vacating one of the seats by sharing the other. Turning around rather aggressively and with no small amount of attitude, she walked right back in my direction, caught me looking at her with some bewilderment, then stopped directly in front of me, just long enough to offer a rhetorical apology in perfectly cultured American English, at the same time announcing she was certain I wasn't going to mind if she sat down across from me, for about half an hour! Truth was, I didn't have any choice, and by now, I was thoroughly amused.

It was clearly evident that her interruption of my seance was not done with malicious intent, but suspend me in the moment she did. She seemed to have some kind of self-proclaimed privileged air about her — that it was somehow unapologetically permissible for her, in all her flamboyance, to dominate the premises for as long as she was here! With that, she managed, rather ungraciously I thought, to plop and wiggle her unshapely buxom self into comfortable position across from me at the café table and, thankfully, put that formidable cane to rest next to her. With sweat beads flowing down her forehead, she expostulated with considerable amperage that it was necessary for her to sit as near to the door as possible while she awaited a new driver, the other having been just dismissed by her for inefficiency. The other twoattendants were sent merrily packing, each with a few rubles from Madame's fat pocket. Taking a deep breath of relief at last, she looked at me, nodding her head slowly but with intention, saying: "Oh my dear, never grow old!"

I smiled, laughed out loud, in fact. I also nodded my head in acknowledgement, but unrehearsed and without contemplation, I couldn't think of anything to say that would easily please her, as if she needed to be told anything. With some amusement, I watched her shift parts of her anatomy from one position to another, while she struggled to pull a beautiful Venetian-looking fan from one of her three leather bags to cool herself. Fortunately, she found a handkerchief in another bag to wipe her furled brow: "My dear, I've just flown in from Helsinki, where I celebrated my eighty-sixth birthday yesterday," she said, "and the party is still going on."

"Oh, how grand! Happy Birthday to you, dear Madame," I finally said to her, not knowing if she was complaining or boasting, or just irritated about everything in general at the moment.

"Thank you very much, my dear. And I would not have flown here in the middle of the party, but it became important and necessary to make this detour to St. Petersburg because of an argument I was having with one of my guests from New York," she offered, though not so happily.

I was watching her with endless delight, when she suddenly inquired: "Now tell me, my dear, are you traveling? Are you alone?"

"Yes, I am from San Francisco, and I'm traveling alone. In fact, I'll be in St. Petersburg for three weeks."

"Good, that's excellent! Traveling with groups of people is absolutely absurd and preposterous. I travel all over the world on my own, especially since my husband's passing, and there is no other way to do it satisfactorily," she lauded, with all the conviction and wisdom she had obviously stored up over her many years.

For the next few moments, while she continued to shift in her seat and dig in her bags, I pondered these words, having always felt very much the same about my own travels, when suddenly, and without warning, she belted out, still rummaging in her bag: "You're a girl after my heart, and I think you should come and visit me in New York some weekend."

It wasn't exactly like we'd known one another for the past several decades, I thought, if even for the past few minutes, but I listened with keen interest as she bantered on: "I have a large four-bedroom penthouse on Park Avenue in Manhattan. It's absolutely empty because I am a widow. I am very rich and a well-known benefactor for the Museum of Modern Art. My husband, once a famous photographer, died many years ago, and I have so much space where I live, I don't see most of it throughout the year!"

While she continued to dig in her bag, without once looking up at me, I observed her with great interest as I tried to size up this curiously novel situation: from San Francisco, halfway around the world, I'm sitting in a hotel loggia in St. Petersburg, minding my own business, and ending up having this dialogue with a complete stranger from New York who has just flown in on a purposeful detour from Helsinki for a reason still mostly unknown to me at the moment.

The hotel bartender brought the glass of bordeaux I had ordered a while back. This caught her attention momentarily, and I offered to buy her a glass as well: "No, no, my dear, but thank you very much. You have class!"

"Thank you, Madame," I said, and then, for the sake of continuing the conversation, thinking that moving on with my postcard writing project would be rude while she was there, I wondered what I should really say next. I got my nerve up to ask, with appropriate apologies, whether she had extended family. She instantly discontinued the search in her bag, and paid attention.

Without a moment's hesitation, she launched into her answer: "Oh my dear, even though it saddens me, I always enjoy talking about my family. I had two very handsome and intelligent sons. One is alive, employed on Wall Street, and a happily married father of my two brilliant grandchildren. The other, my gay son, was killed by a street gang many years ago. Poor dear was only twenty-three at the time!" she reflected, as she cast her sad glance downward, and out the window, momentarily transfixed upon the oversized bronze statue of Peter the Great on his spirited steed, out there in the middle of the largest square in St. Petersburg.

"I'm very sorry to hear this, Madame." Shaking herself free of a long and pensive pause, she began telling me how she had spent the last seven years of her life traveling around the world with much more frequency and vigor than ever before; that while she was still physically able, she was doing what had always fascinated her most. And then, with a mischievous glint in her eye, "Besides, I love to go somewhere and prove my friends wrong!"

She explained that odd remark by telling me about her circle of elite and eclectic acquaintances, her educated Manhattan friends, who, she said, ". . . know everything, even if they don't. Many of them have seldom been out of their penthouses long enough to drive up and down the length of Manhattan!" she groused. She went on to tell me that art and art history had always been her two passions in life.

Back to a persistent search for some item in her bag, she looked up at me, saying: "I don't even know your name; I apologize for my rudeness. I am a little distracted today. What IS your name? Asking your name means I like you. You are smart and beautiful," she insisted, "and you travel alone, which means you are also interesting and, most importantly, you seem curious." That little repartee ended with an impatient hand slap on her sizable thigh, as she looked with some frustration up and down the café corridor, wondering where her designated new driver was.

"Yes, Madame, I'm curious alright!" I said, proudly, and no less confidently.

Then, reaching her puffy little hand across the table, she said: "My name is Anya, Anya von Bulow, a half-Russian aristocrat born in New York."

I'm Erika," I told her, "a gypsy born in Canada."

"That's a pretty name; with a 'k' I would presume? You look German." She wanted to know but didn't wait for an answer.

Growing agitated at whatever it was she had difficulty finding in her bag, plus the non-appearance of her new driver, she complained: "That's precisely why I was forced to fire the previous one! Time is the only thing I don't have any of on this trip. I have come to St. Petersburg specifically today to go to the third room of the Matisse collection in the Hermitage to settle an argument I am having with one of my educated friends from Manhattan about the color of dress the woman is wearing in Matisse's painting entitled "Harmony in Red." She thinks it's red; I know it's black and white, and I know I'm right! The room is red, and there is a green painting on the red wall, but the woman's dress is black and white!"

In disbelief, I burst into laughter. "How wonderful! You can do these things in your life! Fly from Helsinki to St. Petersburg on an afternoon to determine who's correct about the color of a dress in a Matisse painting! How amazing. You are a spirited and fun-loving lady, indeed!" I told her.

"Wonderful, you say. I'm not so sure. I really need to get back to Helsinki at some point today to finish these celebrations. My friends are still all there, and I told them I would be back in time to share the birthday cake which is to be served late this evening. After all, I paid for their hotel rooms, so they can't really leave now," she pronounced, very articulately and confidently, with that adorably pompous demeanor she had. I shook my head in disbelief, loving every minute of this entire exchange.

Having grown sufficiently distressed, Anya was about to pick up her cane and walk toward the door when, thankfully, her driver appeared. A woman in uniform, whom Anya shook hands with, and then told her stiffly but politely, in Russian, to take two of her bags and go back out and wait by the car, and she would be along in a minute. Now that the driver was here, time was back in Anya's control.

She took one more moment to dig in her bag. "Ah, there it is; I thought I had one!" she exclaimed, as she pulled out a wrinkled address card, more or less tossing it onto the table in front of me, and insisting I come visit her in New York, explaining that wherever she traveled around the world, she always invited people to come spend a weekend with her in her beautiful mansion — if she found them worthy of such an invitation!

"But don't wait too long," she cautioned. "I'm not a youngster anymore, and when you come, you will please arrive on a Friday evening; you and I will have cocktails and hors d'oeuvres that evening, we'll breakfast together on Saturday morning, after which you are on your own. You may stay until Sunday evening. Those are the rules. So now make sure you come soon."

She got up, as did I. We exchanged a perfunctory hug, and she waddled off, her body tilting from side to side. A moment before disappearing through the revolving door, she turned back to me with a satisfied grin on her face. "Bye, dear, be well, enjoy your stay in one of the world's most beautiful cities." Out she went, carrying one bag on her left shoulder and her walking cane in her right hand. The driver was still obediently waiting near the car, and promptly opened the door for Anya to climb in, all accessories intact.

I watched Anya wave her fat little hand through the window of her 'hired' Mercedes, and they drove off around the corner toward the Hermitage. And then the impact of this last hour hit me, like the ocean's surf, leaving me breathless in my little nook at the four-star Hotel Astoria, wondering what had just bolted in and out of here. The lovely hostess came round to offer another glass of wine, and I said, "Yes! Please make it the best you have," which she understood and responded to in her cryptic English.

I really wanted to celebrate this wonderful moment. Feeling energized by Anya, an overwhelming mixture of sadness and flamboyance overcame me for the next half hour, thinking about my life and the people in it. I was awed by her conscientious strength, her loyal simplicity, her deliberateness. I felt like a dazzled moth by evening's lamplight. Off in the distant corner of the lobby, I could hear the muffled hiss of the espresso machine that had a little more than an hour earlier produced a great cup of caffeinated mix for me. Anya had been no blue-haired American tingling her bangles at some bar. This was no lofty tourist to be dismissed with a grimace.

My wine glass empty, I gathered up my assorted items and turned to leave, but before doing so, sat down once more, briefly. I smiled as I picked up the name card she had left behind. I wondered, if I looked behind me just now, whether I would see a shimmering presence beckoning with her walking stick, saying: "Come! Come with me!" I didn't dare look. I was afraid I wouldn't see her. I was afraid of being disappointed . . .

~ ~ ~ ~ ~ ~ ~

[I have never visited Anya in New York, sadly, but we have had a most interesting email correspondence during these past eight years. She turned ninety-two this year, responding in typical Anya fashion to a happy birthday wish I sent her, telling me that ninety-two years ago, when she was a few months old, her mother had wheeled her in a wicker carriage from 98th Street in Manhattan down to Times Square for the New York City celebration of Armistice Day on November 11th. "It was 1918. It was the end of World War I, and it was prohibition time," she wrote. In some way, I have always preferred to keep her off in the intriguing colorful distance.]

IV.
FORTUITOUS
HAPPENSTANCE

THE CHARLES BRIDGE

Upon arrival in Prague's city center, I was warmly greeted by my hosts, Jan and Rida Nemeç, whose home, very near Wenceslas Square, I would be renting for two weeks. They invited me in, gave me the necessary orientation, then, before leaving, invited me to sit down for a welcome toast. From the glassed-in bookshelf in the living room, Jan withdrew three little shot glasses and a bottle of very potent Slovakian slivovitz. "It is our custom!" he said. "Welcome to Prague, and to our home. We hope you will be happy here."

"Thank you," I said. "It's a beautiful home, and so many rooms."

With almost excruciating politeness, he explained: "Yes, we have two children still living with us, one is sixteen, a girl named Lenka, and the boy, two years older, is Ianos. Both are now on Summer break from schools, as am I. I am professor of geology at the main university in Prague. In the morning, my wife and I, together with our daughter, will drive to the country for vacation."

"And your son, what will he do?" I asked.

"He will stay with the son of our friends on the other side of the River, and he will try to earn a little money, to help buy his books for university. In Summer, many young people make crafts to sell on the Charles Bridge, others play music with piccolos and accordions, and so on."

I smiled. "Will I discover your son when I cross the Bridge?" I asked.

"Perhaps," Jan replied, and with that, he and Rida excused themselves, and wished me a good stay in their city.

~ ~ ~ ~ ~ ~ ~

I'm never sure what it is about bridges that magnetizes my attention, just like lighthouses do. But I have always enjoyed thinking about bridges as being symbolic, that crossing them from one end to the other is about more than just crossing a river, a thought I have pondered many other times in my life while crossing bridges, in Paris, in San Francisco, in London, in Istanbul. Perhaps here in Prague this time.

During these two wonderful weeks, I saw many things, but what I remember most was the stunning and stalwart stone Charles Bridge stretched across the widest part of the Vltava River which splits the city into two parts. The bridge, commissioned by King Charles IV, was designed by his favorite architect, a German named Petr Parléř, and built in 1357. It is said that the architect insisted that egg yolks be mixed into the mortar to strengthen its construction.

The Charles Bridge was once the most important connection between the Prague Castle and the city's Old Town and adjacent areas. It is a rather wide bridge, and in addition to being the horse and carriage crossing between the two halves of the city, it was also to be a functional area for peaceful equestrian tournaments to allow the knights in armor to display their prowess and chivalry.

Between the 17th and 19th Centuries, thirty statues of saints were created and erected on both sides of the bridge, the most interesting one, if not most important, being the statue of John of Nepomuk, who would become the patron saint of Prague. Poor John was drowned in the Vltava River at the behest of Wenceslaus, King of Bohemia. It is alleged that John, as the confessor of the Queen of Bohemia, refused to divulge the secrets of her confessional. On the basis of this, the King had him thrown off the Charles Bridge and drowned. As a patron against calumnies he was considered the first martyr of the Seal of the Confessional, and because of the manner of his death, John of Nepomuk is considered the saint of protection from floods.

Today the Charles Bridge is a highly celebrated monument, of course, and well-known to thousands of tourists. A pedestrian-only bridge, it is lined with stern and ancient Baroque statues of home-grown saints. The bridge is also a festive gathering place for portrait artists, Peruvian pipe players, trinket stalls and craft vendors, dancing marionettes and accordion players, classical violinists invoking Emperor Franz Josef, and off behind the wooden chairs of their masters, a number of the most docile sleeping whippets — a dog I happen to be very fond of.

Indeed, the Charles Bridge is a living theatre from end to end. Crossing it at day is merely to say you've been there as it is mostly a matter of plowing one's way through. At eventide, it is an entirely different matter. And very romantic, particularly at sunset when one can enjoy a breathtaking view of the fully lit Prague Castle and the entire Prague skyline, against the red evening sky.

On my last evening, I had a lovely dinner at a highly recommended restaurant on the Castle grounds, in what was once the beer brewery. Beautiful brickwork, rounded archways from one section to the next, and at the end of it, the proverbial trickling fountain, with a folkloric angel perched on a rock at the edge of the pond playing his pan flute. Baroque music wafting through the space made it a very perfect setting for tranquil dining and easy ingestion.

After dinner, I walked down the Castle hill to the bridge, wanting to see it by night. It was nearly midnight on a gentle and balmy evening, the well-worn cobbles glistening by the street lantern's light, the statues of the sculpted saints gleaming against a shimmering Vltava River, and overhead, just above the clouds, a glorious sliver of a silver moon still visible.

Strolling along, I could hear the faint sounds of music up ahead. Though this was not Vienna, I and a few other wanderers came upon a group of three musicians playing the strains of Johann Strauss waltzes. I could hardly keep from breaking into a solo one-two-three. I listened to them finish a set and then headed toward the big main gate, called the Gunpowder Tower. And there, at the very end of the bridge, dressed in full costume to look like Mozart, brocaded jacket, white wig, white stockings, the whole ensemble, was a young man performing a slow movement from a Mozart violin concerto, the orchestral accompaniment coming from a tape in his little boombox. I stopped, and along with a half dozen others, we listened to him for a few rapturous minutes, thoroughly enchanted. When he finished, I went up, dropped a few korunas in his violin case, and told him: "You are amazing, you play extremely well, and you are even dressed as Mozart himself."

He bowed broadly, and thanked me. Then he said, "You are American?" I told him I was from San Francisco.

"You speak very good English," I commented. "Where did you learn it? Were you born in Prague?"

"Yes," he said, "I was born right here, near Wenceslas Square. My name is Ianos, and I and my younger sister were taught English in our home. We live with my parents. My father is a geology professor at the university."

My eyes opened wide, my ears perked up, and I couldn't resist: "Is your father's name Jan Nemeç, by chance?"

"Yes," he said, "how do you know him?"

"I stayed in the home of your parents for two weeks, your home," and he smiled from ear to adorable ear. He hoped I would return again the next day, but alas, I was leaving. I was delighted to have experienced this triumphant moment, hearing Ianos play his violin on this ancient cosmos that is the Charles Bridge, making a little Summer money. I was hoping I had contributed toward the purchase of at least one assigned book for his next university semester.

LITTLE YELLOW METRO CAR

BUDAPEST, HUNGARY
August 1996

Budapest is bold, and big! Big palaces, big cathedrals, big buildings, big boulevards, big rooms. She is the undeniable Queen of the incomparable Danube River, which divides her into Buda and Pest, whose glittering Chain Bridge creates a beautiful bracelet that unites the city's two distinct panoramas. She has survived wars and invasions, rebellions and sieges; she was pummeled by the Mongols in the Thirteenth Century, by the Turks in the Sixteenth Century, and by the Soviets during World War II. Finally, slipping nonviolently from the Communist grip in the mid 1950s, she now stands pristine and proud, and very secure in her cultural independence.

~ ~ ~ ~ ~ ~ ~

I arrived in Budapest on a sunny mid-week afternoon, having come by train from Prague in an eleven-hour ride across the lush heathlands of Hungary. I felt like a privileged passenger on the Orient Express as the train eased with noble elegance into Budapest's classically grand Nyugati train station, a fascinating eclectic structure built in the late 1800s by the Eiffel Company.

Stepping off the train was as if heaven's door had opened and served me a loving, warm, motherly, old-world city, covered in regal splendor. Thousands of years of richly interwoven learning and culture, and all of it crowned on the highest rise by a spectacular royal palace, so big one could see its gold rooftops from the train station at the far western end of the city.

A pre-ordered taxi met me at the train station. A beautiful drive brought me to my very prestigious address on the bustling boulevard Belgrad alongside the Danube. A fellow traveler had recommended this very elegant fourth-floor apartment with its full view of the Buda Castle across the Danube. Once we got through a rather undignified lobby, which seemed to be the kitchen's extension of an adjoining goulash restaurant, and clambered up four floors of very rickety wooden stairs, I unlocked a thick wooden door and stepped right into the glow and splendor of old Budapest.

The apartment was the home of a well-known Hungarian artist, and as such very tastefully decorated with his own artwork. The moment I walked into the front parlor, I fully expected Mozart to appear and perform in honor of my arrival. A gigantic and charming old-world room with floor to ceiling windows and thick brocaded drapery. I imagined that long ago every inch of this place would have been gilded, mirrored, and carved. I literally screeched with delight to see a large antique oak desk in the corner, facing the river, with the Castle straight ahead and the Chain Bridge to the right. These would surely be the most inspired postcards I would ever write. Outside, below my window balcony, I could hear what I presumed to be gypsies playing their fiddles and zithers amidst the fuss and flurry of myriad cafés strung along the grand boulevard.

The city seemed an industrious delight, offering magnificent daily thrills. To name a few of the many incredible sights to see: the unavoidable Buda Castle of course, the kilometer-long Royal Palace, the sweeping Parliament Buildings, all of these structures looking like Renaissance paintings in the sky reflected in the silent flow of the Danube, the plume and pride of Budapest. And next to the Castle, the curiously interesting and famous medieval fortification called Fisherman's Bastion, where fishermen had indeed banded together in the Eighteenth Century to defend the ramparts of the city.

~ ~ ~ ~ ~ ~ ~

One of the first outings I planned was a night at the National State Opera House, to watch a very traditional production of Richard Strauss's 'Salomé.' I took the opportunity, before the opera to go to the legendary literary Café Hungaria, to indulge in a mochaccino with one of their very rich pastries: a local specialty and high calorie petite crêpe filled with chocolate, nuts, and cream. Not only was the confection decadent; the interior of the café was literally dripping with deco detail, the kind of place in which I could easily imagine eating one of these cream-stuffed petite crêpes.

Full of energy on a sugar-high, I wandered to the nearest Metro station in order to ride the famous Little Yellow Metro Car, built by the Russians in 1896, and still operating today. Budapest's subway is one of the oldest lines in the world, following the London Underground, built in 1863.

This Little Yellow Metro Car, so small one must duck to enter, is a big tourist attraction, hence also densely populated and ridden with cunning and ingenious pick-pockets. Having read about this, I felt appropriately prepared. Always being out to defy the odds, I naturally had my radar set on high alert all around me. I left my shoulder bag at home, put some paper bills in one of my deep jacket pockets, and my three keys in a leather pouch, which I fastened securely to a wide waist belt I was wearing. This also gave both my hands freedom to hang on during this bumpy, if historical, little ride.

~ ~ ~ ~ ~ ~ ~

The opera was pure joy, as Richard Strauss always is for me. It was now close to midnight, and I found myself strolling happily through the alleys of Pest in search of just the right wine bar for a little nightcap. In complete disbelief, I discovered a Janis Joplin jazz bar, going strong, and I walked in. Everyone recognized me as a non-local, of course; but a name like Janis Joplin was asking for tourists to stop by, certainly the likes of me, from San Francisco. In a thickly accented English, the bartender greeted me pleasantly: "Good evening! May I offer you a beer or a glass of wine?"

"Yes, I would enjoy a glass of Hungarian red wine, if you have it? Thank you."

"Yes, of course we do," he smiled. "May I serve you our favorite, the Hungarian Bikaver Bull's Blood?" I burst into laughter, which he seemed to anticipate, and then he wanted to know where I was from. "Are you German, or are you American?" A question I had been asked numerous times in my travels throughout Europe.

"Actually, I am neither; I am San Franciscan," I said proudly, as I took my first sip.

"Oh," he smiled, "you must like jazz!"

"Yes, I love it."

He went over to the pianist telling him something as he gestured toward me with a smile and in a few moments, the pianist accompanying himself, burst forth with 'California Dreaming' — in English and in my honor. The bartender came back to chat across the bar with me, and I asked, "Do you ever play any Janis Joplin tunes? I don't really know any, but if you do, I would love to hear something, right here in the Janis Joplin jazz bar!"

"No problem; I will ask him to play 'Woman Left Lonely', also for you. Do you know this tune?"

I had no idea, but I enjoyed every note and every word, and it seemed appropriate given I was alone, though not necessarily lonely. At the end of the song, my wineglass empty, I was ready to head home for a good night's sleep, having enjoyed this beautiful and memorable evening. The bartender set me in the right direction to catch the Little Yellow Metro Car once more, and adding, almost as a last minute warning, "Be careful; don't let the pickpockets get you!"

I smiled rather whimsically at him, thinking I'm safe and a street-smart person, so I'll be fine.

The Little Yellow Metro Car was absolutely jammed with midnight revelers all heading home from somewhere, people pressed against people. I only had three stops to go and was relieved to step out of that thick mess of bodies and into the fresh night air. Feeling high on life, I enjoyed a lovely late-night walk the rest of the way back to my building, and couldn't wait to get inside and hit my pillow. And, I might even have a shot glass beforehand of the wonderful Hungarian liqueur the landlord had left for me. Arriving at the great wooden doors of the front of my building at last, I reached for the keys in my little black leather pouch . . . but the pouch was gone!

"Damn pickpockets!" I wanted to scream into the night.

In shock and instant disbelief, I stood still for a few disoriented seconds, drooped my shoulders, and finally just couldn't help but smile at the stealth of these pickpockets. But, in this moment, with no modern conveniences like immediate phone access, it also hit me that this was a much bigger problem than I would have imagined, and very quickly that smile turned to weary tears. Another first for me, the always careful one, always prepared, never afraid. I let out an incredulous gasp. Here, in faraway Budapest, by myself, feeling privately invaded and in a complete quandary, I was forced to admit I had kind of set myself up for it.

Concerned and embarrassed, I stood in my tracks, perplexed beyond belief. The outside tables and chairs belonging to the goulash restaurant on the ground floor had not yet been folded away for the night, so I sat down, to try to regroup and plan my strategy.

This being a Saturday, well past midnight, meant the next day, Sunday, merchants, craftspeople, and small businesses were closed. The landlord of my apartment was gone on holidays to the Black Sea, leaving only the phone number of his friend to call in case of emergency, with the added apology that if it was a weekend, he, too, might well be gone for a ride into the country with his family.

So, my goose was cooked.

To add to the aggravation, a locksmith, once found, would need to pick three separate locks, as each door required a different key, all of which were in that pouch, that probably got thrown into some dark alley with the keys still in it because the pickpocket was after money. Poor guy must have been very disappointed in my pouch!

Watching night revelers coming and going, and thinking about the mess I got myself into, another tenant of the building arrived at the door. I immediately ran up behind him and he let me in, not that that did me any good. He had no keys to the two other doors to my apartment. Anyway, I didn't last very long in that lobby, which was assaulted by an overwhelmingly dank and viscous smell of beef, being boiled, no doubt, for tomorrow's goulash. It really was a stinky humid hallway. The little silk dress I was wearing, as well as my long hair, picked up the fetid scent immediately. There was nowhere to sit that wasn't covered with mucky build-up in that foyer, so I would have to stand up. There were no chairs anywhere to sit on so I thought maybe of propping myself up in the old no-longer-used concierge's box, but it looked a little too much like a church confessional for me to feel comfortable in.

After sizing things up rather negatively, I went to the kitchen, where a cook was still working. With sign language and a few verbal utterances, I was able to explain to him that I was locked out. He could speak a little German, so I was able to better explain my dilemma, but he had no solutions, no keys, and did not know the owner, or how to reach him. He was merely an employee of the restaurant, and the manager was already gone for the night.

It was getting very late, close to two o'clock in the night. I'm not sure why, but I decided to climb the four flights of steps to my door, and hope for magic. Knowing there was another apartment across from mine, I began working up courage to knock on its door. To my surprise, an elderly gent, dressed in a long nightgown and nightcap, opened the door, and facing me in flustered annoyance, his eyes recoiling from the hallway light, he asked, in broken English: "Are you lost? Who are you? You don't live here!"

"I am very sorry, sir. I am occupying the flat across from you, and I am locked out!" I moaned rather apologetically.

He did feel some empathy, and gave me a few suggestions, like perhaps waking the elderly lady one floor down; her son was the caretaker of the building. I thanked him and then, out of curiosity, because he spoke good English, I had the audacity to ask where he was from. With a half smile on his face, he actually told me. "I was born right here in Budapest, but my wife is from New Zealand."

I thanked him, and feeling ever more embarrassed as time ticked onward in this night, I went down to wake up another poor inhabitant, the rationale being that, surely, if they were the caretakers of this building, they would have to expect mishaps like this, but better yet, they would surely have keys to all apartments.

I rang, and waited, and waited. I rang once more, and finally, the creaky door opened about six inches, and from the pitch black darkness within, I could hear a very agitated and gravelly voice grunt at me, in Hungarian. Couldn't say I blamed her, but I muttered something back, while making a motion like a key opening the door, and at last she opened her door and came out into the hallway. I wasn't even sure if she was that mother the gentleman upstairs had referred to. She appeared to be about eighty years old, wearing a very old black nightgown, and a black wrap around her head, hiding what looked like a very weathered face, with a hooked nose, deep set eyes, and no teeth, of course. She gave me a wave of the hand, as if to say get lost, and closed her door to the night. I felt like a stupid orphan, bewildered, not to mention annoyed with myself for all the trouble and unjustified intrusion I had plied the building's inhabitants with.

I gave up and went back down to the sticky lobby; lack of sleep had me caring less about my little silk dress by now, so I sat down, perched my chin in my two hands, and closed my eyes. Fortunately, there was only about an hour left before dawn. In fact, not too long after I settled myself, I was rudely jarred from my trance by a butcher delivering several long and heavy slabs of meat for the goulash restaurant. I had no earthly idea how to interpret the look he gave me . . . nor did I care.

~ ~ ~ ~ ~ ~ ~

The early morning's light was finally peering through, a good indication that it was time for me to get into the fresh air. Here and there, people were beginning to surface. A few gypsies were already strolling about, getting situated for the upcoming day. The inviting smell of brewing coffee began to filter through the air from somewhere. The mighty Danube was just a few feet away, doing her thing, the lights of the Chain Bridge were off, and a lovely dawn was rising in the eastern sky, behind the splendorous Buda Castle.

Glancing around, I was looking to my right, and it suddenly hit me like a bolt of lightening: Why not go to the Duna Intercontinental Hotel next door, which was run by British people, and speak to a concierge at the registration counter. He could surely help by calling the police, or calling a locksmith. In fact, I was annoyed I hadn't thought of that sooner, since this hotel was open all night. On second thought, I wasn't so keen on the police being called, but the locksmith idea was worth pursuing.

The concierge saw me coming and was already smiling. He could tell something was awry. My clothes were all wrinkled and my appearance rather grungy. There was a fairly good chance I probably smelled like boiled goulash, as well. Red-eyed and somewhat abashed, I explained what had happened. Not only did he speak extremely good English, but it just so happened that he had a friend in Budapest who was a . . . locksmith!! Was I in business, or what! I wanted to jump across the counter and hug him.

Before contacting his friend however, he wanted to explain that because it was Sunday, this could be an expensive transaction.

He hesitated, when I asked how much, because the locksmith might have to cut through the locking mechanism, and this could take a while, and perhaps he may not find or have replacement keys with him. All of which was true, not to mention that I was about to ask someone to break into my landlord's apartment. So there were chances and risks involved. But I was willing to pay the consequences. I told him not to worry; I would take full responsibility. And he gave me an estimate of three hundred forints, which was the equivalent of about ten dollars!

I gave him the high sign, he called his friend, and I waited in the hotel lobby for him. Soon, a blond-haired, blue-eyed muscular young man arrived, swinging a very handsome wooden kit by his side. I later saw that this kit contained some even more handsome wooden tools. If only my father had seen those, I thought to myself!

The young man saw me, figured I was the misfit, but greeted me with a warm and amiable handshake, nonetheless, and I could feel I had struck gold with this one. "My name is Gabor," he said in heavily accented English. I told him my story and discovered he understood English reasonably well because he had travelled to England not too long ago; he was, however, reluctant to speak.

We laughed all the way down the boulevard to my building. Once there, the owner of the goulash restaurant agreed to let us into the foyer. So, that was one lock that did not need to be worked through.

We reached the door to my apartment, where he gave the lock a quick and seemingly unconcerned study. I then had the privilege, for about fifteen minutes, of watching a true master at his craft. A very skilled locksmith, an artisan, I thought, as I observed him, humming away, with laser focus, and when he finally and successfully picked the lock, we both shouted in tandem, "Hurrah." He was relieved nothing needed to be cut or sawed or broken, and so was I.

Once inside, the first thing I did was grab my other set of keys, and try the door to make sure all was well! I then invited him in for a beer, but he didn't have time. "More locks to pry open?" I asked, making fun of myself for having been so nonchalant about pickpockets.

"Oh yes, here in Budapest, I am very busy all the time! Locksmithing is full-time work for me," he said, quite innocently.

"It must be because of the smart pickpockets that live here," I joked. "At least they help you earn money!" Gabor smiled in agreement, and then wrote some numbers on a piece of paper which roughly translated into ten dollars for his services. Feeling so much enthusiasm for this man's zest for life, and his conscientious will to help, and realizing what this ordeal would have cost me at home, I paid him triple, hoping it wouldn't upset or embarrass him, and he smiled from side to side.

"I have one child, a son, and I will buy him something special with this. Thank you very much!"

A polite handshake, and Gabor was down the stairs, whistling, and out the door.

~ ~ ~ ~ ~ ~ ~

I, too, went happily down the stairs, keys safely stowed in my shoulder bag, and headed straight for the old Turkish baths up on Gellert Hill, where I spent the rest of my day. Nothing had felt so good in a long time.

ÜSKÜDAR AND SOFIA

ISTANBUL, TURKEY
August 1994

As a young teenager, living a mile from a tiny village situated on the vast central prairies of Canada, I frequently dreamed of visiting big cities in large countries, and preferably beyond my parents' farmyard. I was endlessly thankful for a certain tome on my father's notorious little bookshelf, a collection of Richard Halliburton's extensive travel tales, published in 1937, three years before my birth. Reading this book gave me two things: historical information and, more importantly to my way of thinking, enthusiasm. One of the many places described in the book was the noble mosque Hagia Sophia, in Istanbul, which I hoped one day to visit.

~ ~ ~ ~ ~ ~ ~

I am immediately jumping forty years ahead. I am in Turkey, and I have just endured an insanely endless bus trip from Ephesus in the southwest to Istanbul — a long and arduous journey along bumpy roads, in humid Summer heat with no air conditioning, and with at least a half dozen smokers on board. I have come to this great city to see many things, but mainly Hagia Sofia.

It was nearing sunset, and we still needed to be ferried from the Asian side of Turkey to the European side across the Bosphorus Strait, which connects the Black Sea with the Aegean Sea. A much smaller body of water, the Sea of Marmara, intervenes, creating the beautiful coastline surrounding European Istanbul known as the Golden Horn.

Eventually loaded onto the ferry, we sailed westward, a short half hour across the strait. Along with a few presumably local people, I watched from the upper deck as we neared the magnificent Golden Horn — a scene straight out of Arabian nights, with its forest of tall, thin minarets stretching upward in the ghostly dusk. I was thrilled to be here, in the big magical middle of both Asia and Europe.

Over on the right, an unusually enormous chateau-like structure stood out, twinkling with one thousand lights from a high hilltop. Two youngish gentlemen standing next to me were watching with equal enthusiasm as the shoreline approached. "Excuse me, are you from here?" I wanted to know.

"Yes," the one right next to me said. "I live in Istanbul. I am a student of sculpting at an art academy connected with the Fine Arts Museum, at the bottom of the Golden Horn, which, as you can see, is visible from here. I have been in Ankara studying, and am at last returning home. I am so happy to see all these familiar sights again." He seemed eager to tell me about himself, and I was fascinated.

"So, can you tell me what those lights are, way up on the hill to the right?"

With a glow on his bronzed face, he said: "Yes, that is beautiful Üsküdar, one of the wealthier neighborhoods of Istanbul. It has attractive tree-lined streets with lovely shops, seaside cafés, and many of the oldest wooden houses from the Ottoman Empire still standing. There are lovely terraced gardens that fall to the edge of the Bosphorus, where one can walk and enjoy the stunning views across the Strait. It's a beautiful area; my mother is from there. She is Turkish; my father was Armenian."

I was smiling with delight, thinking how great it would be to take a day trip up there. "And what is that large building, with the many lights, looking almost like a palace?"

"By the way, my name is Oktar!" He shook my hand.

"Nice to meet you; I'm Erika."

"So that large building," he went on to explain, "is the Çamlyca High School for Girls, the most prestigious and largest school for girls in all of Turkey. Teachers once came from America, in the Forties and Fifties, to teach English there to daughters of wealthy parents."

My ears perked up at this bit of information; a long-ago memory was suddenly jolted to the front of my mind. Could this have been the same school where my dear friend Kent had been teaching English in 1956, I wondered silently?

~ ~ ~ ~ ~ ~ ~

Shifting back in time just for a moment, I knew Kent in the early Sixties when I was still in Canada, living in Winnipeg. At the time, he was the manager of the Winnipeg Symphony Orchestra, and I happened to be dating Kent's best friend, the first horn player of that orchestra. Many evenings were spent over dinner in Kent's beautiful home. My attention was consistently drawn toward the creative displays of beautiful and diverse artwork he had amassed from frequent world travels, along with hundreds of books and artifacts accumulated over the years.

On one of his walls hung a cluster of three pencil sketches I liked in particular. Each one seemed to be a town square in a different village, or something similar. Kent explained to me he had asked someone to draw these for him when he was living in Istanbul. One of them, a sketch of a cobbled alley leading to the entrance of a very sophisticated building, he pointed out was the front entrance of the girls' school where he taught. He told me the name of the town at the time, but it meant little or nothing to me then. What stayed with me most was his glowing description of a most unusual life he had been privileged to live in faraway Istanbul, on the historical Bosphorus Strait.

Time went on for about thirty years, and so did my life. Kent and I remained in sporadic touch, enough to know where we were each living, I eventually in San Francisco, and he in Halifax, Nova Scotia, where he was now teaching architecture at the University. Our notes crossed mostly at holiday times, when I was always delighted to receive his beautifully hand-penned one-page greetings on parchment.

~ ~ ~ ~ ~ ~ ~

Reverting back to Istanbul, I decided to postpone Hagia Sofia on my calendar to a few days later and, to quell my curiosity, interrupt my sight-seeing sequence with a one-day visit to this seemingly interesting place — Üsküdar. A ferry dropped me at the little dock below the town, and I began climbing up the hill to do some discovering. Once there, it seemed all estate buildings were tightly secured and heavily guarded by large fences, so there was no opportunity to see anything beyond what I could easily see from the shoreline. But I was enchanted, and could not help thinking about Kent the entire time, wondering if by coincidence I had found the place where he once taught. I was almost anxious to get home now and try to reach him in Halifax.

~ ~ ~ ~ ~ ~ ~

Meanwhile, as mentioned, I had come to see much more of Istanbul and its environs, primarily of course the noble Hagia Sofia. My temporary living quarters, directly behind the back side of the mosque, in the very prestigious and newly renovated Ottoman era apartments inside the enormously thick Topkapi Palace walls, gave me several opportunities to walk by The Venerable Old Lady (as Hagia Sofia is affectionately referred to), as I gradually got up my courage to step into her ancient and historical world.

At one end of this old cobbled pedestrian alley was a lovely café, set in Mozartian Rococo, with appropriate chamber music filling the space and flowing out of its shuttered windows onto the plaza. Here, in the sunny courtyard of its pavilion, surrounded by a plenitude of flowers and blossoming bougainvillea, I had the pleasure of continental breakfast every morning — Turkish coffee, and crisp biscuits with yoghurt and honey, in the grand shadow of Her Serene Highness, Hagia Sofia.

One of the unusual pleasures for me on this first visit to the world of Islam was to be awakened at five o'clock every morning, even amidst the omnipresent haggling clatter and noise, by the muezzin greeting the rising sun, and chanting his mantra from the eastern-most minaret of the Hagia Sofia, invoking not only the faithful to prayer, but dogs to howling everywhere.

~ ~ ~ ~ ~ ~ ~

I had been told that the best time of day to visit fifteen hundred-year-old Hagia Sofia was a later hour in the day, to stroll and wander through while the setting sun cast its golden glow upon the amazing features of her grand interior, or to pass through during a full moon, when lunar beams stream through her windows high above, creating an unbelievable sight.

Waiting for the self-appointed hour, I thought it would be a good idea to sit down on a nearby stone bench and read the encapsulated version of her history which I had prepared at home, so I could gain the total impact of this once-in-alifetime visit.

Hagia Sofia, or 'Ayasofya', as the Turks call her, means 'holy wisdom.' From the date of her dedication in 360 A.D., until 1453, she served as the Greek patriarchal basilica of Constantinople, with a brief intermittent conversion to a Roman Catholic cathedral. In 1935, she was opened as a secularized museum.

Famous in particular for her massive dome, Hagia Sofia is considered the epitome of Byzantine architecture and is said to have effectively changed the entire history of world architecture. She was the largest cathedral in the world for nearly one thousand years, until Spain's cathedral-mosque complex in Seville was completed in 1520.

The structural statistics of Hagia Sofia are almost beyond comprehensible proportions. She was constructed under the aegis of Emperor Justinian, who chose a physicist and a mathematician as architects, and employed sixteen thousand builders to complete the task. Materials were demanded, forced, and delivered from across the empire. Shiploads of riches from Athens and Rome. Hellenistic columns from the Temple of Artemis at Ephesus. Large stones from quarries in Egypt, and green marble from Thessaly in central Greece. Black stone came from the Bosphorus region, and yellow stone from Syria.

Justinian, himself, bought forty thousand pounds of silver and half a million pearls just for the altar. And when the building costs left the treasury empty, history tells us, Justinian merely seized the salaries of all state officials, closed schools, and made the army serve without pay. On the day of dedication, with one thousand priests assembled, alongside great choirs and musicians, Justinian declared he had surpassed even King Solomon in displaying the greatness of his temple. Once built, this new basilica was contemporaneously recognized across the planet as the premier monument to Byzantine civilization.

In the year 1130, a French historian, passing through with the Crusaders, exclaimed Hagia Sofia to be "a paradise of beauty, the throne rising to the heavens, and a marvel of the earth." In the early 1500s, Sultan Mohammed came along and claimed it for his mosque, stripping it of all Christian symbols, and spreading verses from the Koran over the pictures of saints. Justinian's pearls and silver from the altar were given to the Sultan's officers, and at each of the four corners outside, a minaret was erected. It was not difficult to realize that Santa Sofia had already endured many levels of war and history long before Columbus ever discovered America.

Colorful descriptions of her life and struggles abound. For fifteen hundred years, numerous luminaries, historians, architects, artists, physicists, researchers, and philosophers have collectively proclaimed that every square inch of her has at one time been fought over, conquered, and reconquered. Sofia has been sacked and plundered; she has been administered over by tyrants and demons, and converted by fanatics and zealots; she has been decimated by both civilized and savage hordes, and her remains carried off by the mules of the crusading captors and ransacking Christian soldiers.

~ ~ ~ ~ ~ ~ ~

At about eight o'clock on a balmy and brightly moonlit evening, I strolled over to visit Her Greatness, to touch her sandstone red walls, study her faded frescoes and tiles, and walk where emperors and peasants had walked through the centuries.

Almost as if on tiptoe, in an undeniably elated state of mind, I approached her main entrance and stepped into the courtyard, which was quite deserted. Slowly, and with considerable effort, I was able to pull open the enormous carved wooden doors and step into the foyer. In the hushed ambience of the sub-entrance, I crossed the ancient and time-worn threshold, stepped through two bronze relief doors, and voilà, directly into the deafening silence of a temple almost too mighty, soaring and stretching upward as if to infinity. Hagia Sofia, The Great Protectress, unhindered by her size, floating upon a crown of colorless windows, thick marble columns holding her aloft. Slowly, I moved to stand directly under her dome, two hundred feet up and one hundred feet wide, a vastness of untouchable magnificence. Acres of space ahead of me and all around me, and so far upward my naked eye could not determine what it was looking at. Dumbstruck by the moonbeams streaming through the windows from the top of the dome, I wanted to send out a benediction in every direction. It was as if someone had actually painted the sky and lowered it a little to fit into this amazing structure.

Even though she is ageless, Hagia Sofia has aged well. Her scars add to her beauty, her nicks and bruises add to her richness; she is faded but brilliant. Though she is an empty vessel, she has a full heart. Though she has consistently been patched, fixed, and repaired since time immemorial, she remains an ancient mother, a goddess, a warm place.

I was grateful for a most sublime visit; my adventurous spirit was elevated to levels heretofore unknown to me.

~ ~ ~ ~ ~ ~ ~

Sadly, it was time to leave behind unforgettable memories and travel home to San Francisco, where I set about the following day eagerly trying to contact my friend Kent in Halifax. The University of Nova Scotia's Architecture Department informed me he had retired nearly five years ago, and then, after listening to my story, decided to give me his telephone number. Fingers shaking with nervous excitement, I dialed the number and a rather formal female voice answered: "Hello, this is the residence of Kent Hurley. How may I help you?"

My heart sank ever so slightly. Somewhat fearful of what else I might hear, I nevertheless said: "I am Erika, a long-ago acquaintance of Kent's from the Winnipeg years, and I once dated his friend from the symphony. I was just in Istanbul and I remembered Kent telling me about a girls' school he taught at. I think I may have been right in the very suburb where he taught but I'm not sure. I wanted to share this excitement with him, and it would also satisfy my curiosity greatly to know for sure." I could sense the lady listening, but not being so immediately responsive.

"Oh Erika," she slowly began, "you and I have never met, but my name is Beatrice, and I'm so very sad to tell you, Kent passed away suddenly two days ago!"

I was completely shocked, and needed a few seconds to collect myself mentally. Beatrice then told me everything that had happened. She had known Kent for many years, including all about his amazing life. She was the executor of his estate, she said, and then she asked for my full name and address. "Perhaps I'll find something in his belongings I think you would enjoy having," she said.

I was stunned, but decided to let this entire thing evolve as it wished.

About three months passed and I had more or less forgotten about the whole situation. Then a big package arrived from an address in Canada unfamiliar to me. When I saw that it was from Nova Scotia, I fell limp, and wondered if it might be from Kent's estate. I opened it, and found inside one of the pencil sketches I had admired years ago in that cluster of three on the wall of his home in Winnipeg. It was that sketch with the cobbled alley leading to the entrance of a very sophisticated building. In the lower right hand corner was the identification: 'Üsküdar.'

The only clue I had given Beatrice was about Kent's teaching at a girls' school. She must have known immediately it was 'Üsküdar.' Also included in the package were a few postcards exchanged between Kent and the first horn player whom I had long ago dated.

THE MYSTERIOUS RAINDROPS OF VALLEDEMOSA

MALLORCA, SPAIN
March 1998

This story will combine and connect three different events occurring within a time span of forty-seven years. I want to call it a symbolic allegory of justice, involving a book, a piano composition, and a long journey to a faraway island. It is also, in part, about the eternal fugitive in me, constantly on a quest for answers, loving the world whenever it takes me around a temporary time-twisting bend, serendipitously bringing together meanings and reasons, for situations caused by completely normal circumstances elsewhere.

I did not know as a child — even though I was already setting the stage for part of it — that of all the ways in which the Universe presents itself, coincidence is one of the most intriguing. Also the most satisfying!

~ ~ ~ ~ ~ ~ ~ ~

It was the Summer of 1951; I was eleven years of age, and thoroughly enjoying the holidays away from school, sitting under the low-hanging branch of that favorite tree behind my mother's potato patch, writing the first queries of an inquisitive mind into my young teen's diary — a little three-by-five booklet with about fifty lined pages and a pressed cardboard cover, upon which was a painted image of a perfect young girl wearing a thinly woven white dress with a blue sash. And by coincidence, or perhaps not, she had wings.

At supper one evening, my father announced that at school's beginning, he would from now on be taking me and my younger sister to a small town twelve miles down a gravelly road for weekly piano lessons. We were to be tutored in the art of classical piano for the next several years by a professional pianist from Utrecht in Holland. A rather stern Dutch Reformist immigrant, Wilhelmina Giessen, a true-blue Victorian in her own right, was already sixty years of age when she arrived on the prairies of rural southern Manitoba with her daughter, recently married to a Canadian soldier returning from a military service base in Europe.

From almost the first piano lesson onward, Mrs. Giessen's rigorous tutelage paid off in that it revealed much sooner than anticipated that my skills on the full keyboard were unusually advanced. After several years under her implacable musical thumb, she pronounced to my proud parents I was more than capable at age fourteen of taking on some of the early though no less challenging piano repertoire of Monsieur Frédéric Chopin and insisted I learn one of his moderately ambitious préludes for a final recital. Exacting and demanding though it was for the hands of a fourteen-year-old, nothing was considered impossible by Mrs. Giessen's standards and expectations. The piece was entitled 'The Raindrop Prélude.'

It took a number of weeks, coupled with Mrs. Giessen's staunch discipline, to achieve her desired ultimatum of my learning to play this prélude from memory. Along with that, of course, were the expected expressions and necessary romantic inflections which, fortunately, I was a natural at. I was thoroughly enjoying this grown-up experience! But there was another dimension included in my excitement about this particular piece. The more I rehearsed it, the more I began to hear the raindrops elicited by the opening bars of its music. The more I could hear the raindrops, the more curious I grew, through my wandering and wondering teenaged mind, about the circumstances of this particular composition.

It wasn't as if I couldn't put my own imagination to work and make up a reason, but in the final stages of rehearsing it a few days before the public recital, I looked into the formidable eyes of my venerable teacher and dared to ask my burning, if innocent, question: "Mrs. Giessen, why did Chopin call this piece 'The Raindrop Prélude'?"

With some surprise at my audacity, she glanced down at me with those portentous eyes, right through her wire-rimmed glasses perched on that long hooked nose, and very curtly pronounced: "Oh my dear Üreka, you are too young to understand such a story; perhaps one day when you are grown up, you will discover it." And then she tapped my hand with her pencil, politely but purposefully, and we continued the rehearsal.

I was not only even more curious now, but also puzzled. That was not an easy response for my restless teenaged spirit to digest; it was, in fact, rather irritating. How dare she tell me something like that, and then leave it dangling in front of me like an out-of-reach carrot in front of a horse. What could there possibly be about the history of a beautiful piece of music, written to imitate the sounds of nature, that wasn't for me to know about now? After all, Mrs. Giessen had always had a story for every Beethoven Sonatina I ever learned under her aegis, so why, I wondered, was I not told the story about this particular Chopin prélude. I pondered it many times; I even arrived at my own secret hypothesis.

~ ~ ~ ~ ~ ~ ~

The final piano recital evening was upon us. I was the last item on the program of four piano graduates from Mrs. Giessen's class, and I played the piece masterfully, on a new upright piano, in a white church on the main street of a small town named Boissevain in Manitoba. A rousing applause. And then Summer followed once more, with its usual out-of-school fun and activities. I eventually forgot about this mysterious prélude and its apparently even more mysterious circumstances.

It was 1955, the Summer I turned fifteen.

~ ~ ~ ~ ~ ~ ~

In the early Autumn of 1955, I was back in Petersburg School, the functional little one-room country school house with one teacher, nine students (one per grade), and one bookshelf at the back of the classroom, mostly hidden from daily view by our outdoor wear having to hang above it.

With full-on enthusiasm, I returned to my beloved wooden desk with its inkwell and drawer for papers. One day, I headed right back to that seemingly insignificant bookshelf to see what I could find. A small book with a French title caught my fancy. The little volume, already translated into English, bore the unassuming title of 'La Petite Fadette,' written by a man named George Sand. The title, as the Introduction explained, could be idiomatically translated into 'The Little Cricket,' or even 'The Little Fool.' It told the story of a spellbinding character dressed in black, with a touch of sorcery and magic, all in one.

Though a metaphoric title for the lead character in the story, I chose the book for the very word 'cricket' because it reminded me of the wonderful creatures I was so familiar with growing up, listening to them during long Summer evenings while lying in the tall oat grasses on the farmyard. Crickets sang happy songs. They were chirpy reminders of innocent fun and, especially, as the days became shorter and cooler, they provided assurance that the grass would grow again next Summer and flowers would sprout, on that little slope behind our unpainted three-story Charles-Addams-mystery-house-look-alike farmhouse.

I read this spellbinding pastoral novelette in its entirety, discovering that it was the first of a series of five Sand had written, one for each grandchild upon its arrival. Just before returning the book to the school shelf at the end of that Autumn, I went back to read what I considered to be the boring part, the Preface, which, at that age, never held any interest for me. But read it I did. To this day, I'm not sure if I would have felt differently about the book suddenly realizing: 'Wait! It says something here about this 'woman' named

George Sand!' Immediately, I wondered, 'What was 'she' doing with a name like George?' After school, I sauntered up to the school teacher's desk and asked her. She had no idea whatsoever, she said! "Then where did this book come from; how did it land on our little country school bookshelf?" I wanted to know. She had no answer for that either.

"Perhaps one day you will discover the answer," she offered, leaving me with even further discontent. Another of life's mysteries to be unraveled . . . and in the inimitable manner of my dear piano teacher, Mrs. Giessen, apparently only when I became an adult.

It had, now on two very different occasions, become clear to me that my curiosity was not being given answers it craved, to anything anywhere. My imagination had no other choice but to grow even more wild with conjecture. Why were there mysteries and secrets and hidden things, just because I was not yet an adult? And besides, what age finally and legally constituted adulthood anyway? It just didn't seem fair that, no matter how many questions, no matter how often I wondered, I would henceforth be continually expected to grow up and learn about life, later. To have learned that George Sand was a woman was very intriguing and I felt compelled from that year on, indeed stirred, toward trying to discover why she had taken a man's name. Furthermore, I felt motivated to finally unravel some of this secrecy that had begun to surround so much of my life.

It would be a while, but these two mysteries would by serendipitous coincidence head straight toward a collision course down the road of my adventurous life.

~ ~ ~ ~ ~ ~ ~

In 1958, I had my eighteenth birthday; I at last found myself all grown up and had, hopefully, become a legitimate adult! I did all the right things. I left the farm, I moved to a big city named Winnipeg, and I did what every oldest child of a farming family on the prairies was more or less expected to do: find a sales clerk job in the city to earn money to send home.

Until this time in my life, the biggest city I had ever been in was a town fifty miles north of my father's farm, with a population at the time of about twenty-five thousand. Walking around on my own now in a busy metropolis of two hundred and fifty thousand people was like wandering around in a huge candy store; I was fascinated. And it didn't take long to discover one of my favorite features: a public library! This gave me tremendous satisfaction, tremendous opportunity, in fact, to learn so much beyond what farm life already had. Even though clouds and trees and Summer grasses and crickets provided some answers, here, in a magical city, I had suddenly arrived in a kingdom of books that were free for me to pull off the shelf, open up, and read randomly through endless pages. Oh how I loved smelling the ink and paper, the oldness of a book, its parchment pages printed on a letter press. It was a deliciously gratifying time for me. I was shivery with joy every time I entered the library's premises.

Once reasonably familiar with this wonderful world of books, I began the hunt for facts and historical lore about this notorious woman with a man's name. In attempting to do research on her, I began to realize how remote she really was; bookstores were selling no books written by her, and even a library this size had no information about her.

It was then it occurred to me that she had written that little novelette one hundred and fifty years ago and that her books were therefore probably long out of print. That didn't please me, but I was not to be held back in my zealous search for information about George Sand, though it made me wonder even more how that book landed on that little country school's bookshelf. My imagination, of course, formulated an opinion: like a tiny seed blown by the winds across land and sea, it had settled there at last, and grown into its own life, ready to become something for someone.

And that someone was me.

~ ~ ~ ~ ~ ~ ~

Over the next two and one-half decades, I moved about the country, the continent, and the world, due somewhat to various kinds of employment, but mostly due to lifestyles and dreams; the ongoing quest to learn more about George Sand continued throughout that time. I began to discover used book stores, and was overjoyed to finally find a few books, written both about her and by her. Further explorations led me to the wonders of book finders. Long before computers with internet assistance and amazon.com, never mind Google, there were endless letter and telephone exchanges that ostensibly helped me find Sand's works, in print and out of print, translations of her novels, and primarily her published memoirs and journals. Ultimately, I purchased anything that had her name on it

It was in all that searching that I discovered George Sand had been a well-known and notorious Nineteenth Century French novelist and memoirist named Amandine Lucile Aurore Dupin, Baroness de Saxe Dudevant, thankfully best known by her pseudonym, George Sand. Discovering, little by little, her nontraditional lifestyle, at a time when my own life was very much bound by conservative religious beliefs and confined by generations of austere family tradition, would have a lasting effect on me; she would become my unconventional and off-beat guide, and my life-long mentor. Born a genuine and nonconforming dilettante, George Sand was about to make one of me.

Eventually, I found a real cache of her works at the Chicago University bookstore. In my ardent desire to collect her works, especially now that I realized they were not so readily available, I finally took another grown-up leap, going about one hundred dollars into debt, and ordering every book they had by and about her, among them — and significant to this story — one of her memoirs entitled: 'Winter in Mallorca.'

~ ~ ~ ~ ~ ~ ~

Fast-forwarding to 1984, I was now forty-four years in age and living in San Francisco. I had begun entertaining thoughts of traveling to southeast Spain, primarily along the Valencia coast, and then ferrying across to Palma on the island of Mallorca, to visit friends.

Remembering Sand's little Mallorca memoir, I took it with me one rare sunny day, found a bench to sit on in Golden Gate Park, and read it, thoroughly enjoying and taking note of her beautiful descriptions of this quaint place, dreaming about being there myself. And then, reading along, about midway into the book, I suddenly gasped out loud. There it was, out of the big blue, and to my complete surprise and overwhelming elation — the big revelation about the events and circumstances surrounding 'The Raindrop Prélude' by Chopin! The person sitting on the other end of the bench heard me react: "Good book?" she wanted to know.

"If only you knew," I said, completely ecstatic, and so, so relieved, if not content at long last. If only Mrs. Giessen were still alive! I would have run to the nearest telephone booth and called her up immediately.

I sat there for a reflective moment with the best smile on my face, feeling very pleased. In all her puritanical and virtuous ways, what the stalwart Mrs. Giessen hadn't wanted to tell me, at the young and 'innocent' age of fifteen, was that Chopin wrote this little prélude during the Winter he spent in Mallorca living communally — or as she would have said it, 'in sin' — with George Sand, in three small rooms of an ancient and defunct monastery in the village of Valledemosa, situated on the western Mediterranean shore, above an olive grove, way up in the mountains just northwest of Palma!

All the pieces were at last falling into place. Whatever the symbols and meanings, whatever the analysis, divine permission or not, I was gratified to have discovered this little piece of history on my own and by pure coincidence.

The story goes that the two left Paris to take Chopin away from the rainy and wet Paris Winter, and bring him to a warmer climate in hopes of curing him of incipient tuberculosis, which he was already suffering from at the time of the move.

Chopin had named this piece 'The Raindrop Prélude' because he composed it one evening when rain was falling during a thunderstorm, and he could hear the drops pattering on the resonant terra-cotta tiles of the roof. That's all. A sweet story! A beautiful story. A perfect story! The loving circumstances of his life with George Sand — which would be the perfect inspiration to compose such naturally soaring music.

~ ~ ~ ~ ~ ~ ~

I stayed sitting on that park bench in Golden Gate Park for a while to think about things. In reflecting back upon the years of my early youth, while struggling with the usual meanings of life and the challenges of existence within a confined and sparse community, that same life was thankfully also interspersed with auspicious and rewarding antidotal moments. George Sand, as I saw it now, had provided a few of those moments for me. The dilettante was happy and alive and living in San Francisco.

At long last, something had come full circle. And my personal and moral mythology could now be re-set to continue its fortification against attempts by my superiors to provide potentially false answers before there were any explanations.

~ ~ ~ ~ ~ ~ ~

And now, to the year 1998, which has me at a full-blown forty-eight years. Having already walked in many of Sand's beguiling and daring footsteps across Europe, I was eager to try to get an even deeper sense of the essence of her life, of her wandering spirit, and, as she grew older, her reasons for doing the things she did with the people she did.

After an incubation period of a little more than a decade, a special pilgrimage was finally about to transpire to that remote mountain village, on the island of Mallorca in the warm Mediterranean. In the Spring of that year, on one balmy and cloudless day, under a pink-tinged late afternoon sky, the jumbo jet hit the tarmac on Mallorca with a grand thump, and so did my heart.

My dear British friends, Barrie and Marion, long-time citizens of Mallorca, greeted me at the airport and brought me to the once ancient Roman camp now known as the city of Palma, to their beautiful small ville maison in the heart of the city. Barrie had been a distinguished headmaster of the international school in Munich, Germany, when I worked for him in the early Seventies, and it was wonderful to see him and his wife again. The evening turned into a lively and typically festive Spanish celebration under a very orange full moon. Mediterranean paella dishes were the culinary indulgence of the moment, and spicy sangria flowed freely all night long. I was enthralled to be in this faraway place.

~ ~ ~ ~ ~ ~ ~

The infamous monastery was now not much farther away. The morning after my arrival, I rented a little car, and took off into the day. The road to the monastery was a long and rather treacherously winding drive up very steep slopes. Reaching the top, I was able to leave the car in a small parking area and, continuing uphill, walk a few hundred steps along a cobbled path toward the monastery's entrance.

At the top, I came upon a small village plaza, and off to one side of it, I could see the gray stone monastery, looking almost forlorn on its time-worn perch. I pushed a typically cyclopean carved wooden double door, creaky on its antiquated hinges, and it opened to the welcome coolness of the interior. Finally, I was about to cross the portal, and step through the very door which had been Sand's and Chopin's own sub-entrance to their apartment. I tried to visualize them doing just that. Slowly, and almost secretly, I then proceeded down the long corridor to their once-residential rooms. And then I heard it: the music, the piped-in piano sounds of Chopin's 'Raindrop Prélude' wafting down the ancient hallway. I stopped in the semi-dark hallway and listened, remembering my own performance of it several decades ago, a long, long way from where I was now.

Within a few moments, and with the proudest steps I had taken in a long time, I entered the domain of Sand and Chopin. I recall the almost fevered excitement of standing where they both had stood, walking where they both had walked. Listening to Chopin's piano music all during the visit brought the whole experience realistically close to what it must have been for them so long ago.

Cautiously and prudently, and in total awe, I advanced into a central common room. On one side Chopin's old and somewhat beaten up Pleyel piano, which had endured a painstaking and long journey by freighter from Paris all those years ago, and now still standing right there, and still upright against the wall. I stared at it for a moment with an enormous urge building in me. I wanted to touch those piano keys in the worst way. No one was watching; I could not resist aiming for the D-flat minor chord (the key of the prélude) and touching the keys; I could hear that familiar chord in my heart, in my pulse, in my head.

Directly opposite, in the same room, was Sand's small wooden writing table, the inkwell now dried up, and the quill on its side and at rest. Ahead, toward the backdoor exit with its view to the gardens, a carved wooden divider hid a small kitchen area. To my right, through a narrow doorway, was Chopin's personal room, and to my left was Sand's.

I took time to wander through these rooms, imagining all kinds of things, looking here and there and all around, before finally stepping out to the gardens, which were sloping gently down on the back side of the monastery toward steep coastal cliffs, at whose feet the Mediterranean was pounding and corroding, just as she had described it all.

It was almost a melancholy feeling being here, seeing the slopes lined with varied tints of oak trees, carob trees, pine, poplar, cypress, and a generous scattering of the omnipotent olive tree. What unfathomable depths of greenery, adorned by torrential visual plunges through groves of lavish leafy exuberance and incomparable grace! And the Moorish terraced mountainsides, dotted here and there with little Arab mud cottages, now empty but still perched on ledges and precipices half hidden among jointed prickly pears, dominated by tall palm fronds leaning over the chasm, and silhouetted black against the day's rosy-colored sky.

I was ecstatic, realizing what had so inspired Sand that entire Winter. To my right, a sublime setting of bold mountains fringing the distance as far as the eye could make out, stretching across the plain, and beyond that, watching the mountain mists begin to rise and cast their transparent veil over the depths in the foreground. One of those overwhelming views that leaves nothing to be desired. Whatever poets and painters might dream, Nature had created it here; vast general effects, countless detail, inexhaustible variety, blurred shapes, bold outlines, hazy depths, not a thing was missing. Looking over the garden wall, I could see exactly what Sand saw, nearly one hundred and fifty years ago.

~ ~ ~ ~ ~ ~ ~

And so it was, here, that the notorious mystery unfolded itself, in this old monastery, established in 1399, on top of these mountains surrounded by the Mediterranean, where Sand had lived with her dear Frédéric, and with her two children, Maurice and Solange. She wrote endlessly in her diary about picking flowers and gathering seeds in the olive groves below, and I would be willing to believe that many of the trees and shrubs in the garden directly behind their living quarters grew from the seeds planted by her own hand.

I was so pleased to know that the rooms once inhabited by Sand and Chopin were now established as a museum in memory of that Winter. Much of the original furniture was there. Happily, I was able to see many of Sand's original manuscripts and Chopin's hand-scripted music sheets, behind the locked glass lid of a bookshelf. Sand's bank account book was also there, in full view, accompanied by detailed and painstaking descriptions of all her expenses and their related histories, in her own beautiful and inimitable script, every capital letter swirling as if an adorning piece of corner lace on a tablecloth. Here in these tiny living cells — as she called them — was the closest I would get to her, at least in this place. My dear mentor, so long gone, though always alive and present in my mind.

An interesting side note, for me, was that this museum installation and the maintenance of it had all been made possible through the generous support of several generations of a wealthy Mallorcan family still living in Palma today, and whose ancestor was one of the monks in that monastery when it was functioning as such many centuries before.

~ ~ ~ ~ ~ ~ ~

Fortunately, during my stay in Palma, I was able to make two trips to Valledemosa. I wanted to drive up this winding road once more, to go back and sit on the rock bench built into the garden wall overlooking the olive orchard below. I wanted to write a letter to George, seal it in an envelope, and leave it on her writing table. I wrote the letter into my journal as well, so as to have a 'copy' of it. In part, it said:

Monday, March 30, 1998

My Dear George,

As I walk through your cell here in this ancient Carthusian monastery, high above Palma, in the cloud-covered mountains of this day, I am very happy — you have moved me toward confidence with your strong conviction and determination. As I walk on the tiles you walked on a century and one-half ago, I feel you. I wonder how you were on this day, in 1838-39? How uplifting it has been to feel your presence, to know that you were once here. Your courage gives me hope and faith.

I will never set foot here again, but [on this visit] I have tried to take you with me in every way. Your script, your writing, your photographs, your sentiment, your indomitable spirit, never to be vanquished. Today, I am here alone; no one is babbling around me — and I hear the sensuous notes that dear Frédéric composed under this roof. I have at last found the essence of what constituted the composing and creation of his beautiful "Raindrop Prelude" — which I once performed with all the passion a fifteen-year-old can muster — a fifteen-year old whose wings were eager to fly into infinity with feelings unfettered and desires acknowledged.

How wonderful it has been to be here, in your home, close to you. I adore you. You have been a mentor to me since I was a young child. I thank you now as I kiss the rock wall where you assuredly must have stood, looking, wondering as I am now, feeling things, feeling so much not definable, not describable, not mentionable. I have picked a rose petal from your garden, to press in my journal, just as you taught me; and I have taken a seed from your rosemary bush; perhaps it is one that will sprout in my own garden, and be the continuation of your legacy, of everything you stood for. To disappear from sunlight into a dark monastery and enter back into the light which covered you for one Winter in Mallorca, right here where I stand, is the only memory of you I need. I am separated here from all who know me, except you. You had a dream, and you did something about it. You cared, and it showed.

I have admired you for so many years, and do so even more now. You have inspired me to become the next 'notorious woman', in your own inimitable George Sand way. I have followed your muse with great enthusiasm and keen interest, and I have adopted you as my primary role model and life mentor, particularly in journal writing, which you tantalized, realized, and finalized for me in a big and influential way.

Thank you for teaching me the ways of universal living and thinking.

I love you, as a kindred spirit, Erika

~ ~ ~ ~ ~ ~ ~

On the way out of the monastery, the second time, I stopped in a little gift boutique to purchase a CD of some more of the music Chopin had composed during that Winter in Valledemosa. The greater portion of these works, I found out, were performed by him, after returning from Mallorca, as the featured artist in his most memorable concert at La Salle Pleyel in Paris on April 26, 1841. He was thirty-one years of age, with less than a decade to live.

According to several historians, the evening was an unequalled triumph. The artist, Eugene Delacroix (also famous for painting George Sand's portrait), had stayed in bed for two days to get over a sore throat just so he could attend this concert. Also present were the composers Hector Berlioz and Franz Liszt. Heinrich Heine, the German poet, was there and, of course, George Sand. Whenever I play this CD, I am at that concert, all those years ago.

~ ~ ~ ~ ~ ~ ~

This was a very special journey for me, combining, as I mentioned at the outset, three important elements of my life: the writings of George Sand, the music of Frédéric Chopin, and travels to Mallorca.

And I should not forget to pay my respects to the incorrigible Wilhelmina Giessen.

V.
THE GREAT WHITE CONTINENT

FROZEN STILLNESS

PORT LOCKROY, ANTARCTICA
December 2010

Frozen whiteness
yawning to the horizon

Deep-frozen air
which human skin and eyeballs can't endure

Empty silence
reaching for the mountaintops

White mountains
soaring to twilight-painted skies

No sound
only wind wailing
ice cracking

Deep blue shadows lurking
where ice buckles and breaks

White ice
fathoms deep

Translucent blue ice
enclosed in mountainside caverns

Below white ice
the darkest waters on the planet
where light has not reached
in millions of years

Above white ice
a steel-gray sky
extinguishing a flaming sunset

Under white ice
water moving in giant swells
carrying earth's largest coldblooded mammals

Daylight uninterrupted
month after month

Dark sky
pierced by frozen light of a distant universe
indifferent to human existence

Dry valleys
screaming winds sculpting moonshapes
out of black rock

No roads
no cars
no houses
no people
no footsteps

And the aurora borealis dances unseen

In Silence Beyond Silence

The evolution of this journey to Antarctica had its origins in my early teens. We — that is, my parents and my siblings — were living in the frozen arctic tundra, in Central Canada, on a bleak and flat acreage of stony farmland. Survival was highly dependent upon consistent imagination and self-sufficiency, as well as vigilance and full-on attention to everything beneficial to our wellbeing in a climate which, except for the many daily farmyard chores, kept us indoors more than half the year. My parents, being true and innovative architects of their family, found unfailing ways to brighten our days, even throughout those impoverished years — something my restless youth really appreciated, particularly during long and very cold Winters when the sun was barely up before school and already down immediately after school, and the entire family was then confined to the kitchen for the evening where, by the light of a coal-oil lamp and the warmth of a wood-burning stove, Dad would help us learn multiplication tables while Mom washed up the supper dishes.

From a very early age, I dreamed of venturing away from this grim place. Mom and Dad had one Christmas given me and my siblings an old one-room-schoolhouse globe that twirled conveniently on its stand, and from which I could study and try to memorize the shapes and names of all continents and oceans.

As well, and much to the delight of my insatiable curiosity, especially in areas of geographic and natural sciences, my father decided to submit to the purchase of a twenty-five-year subscription to *Life Magazine*, which subsequently became my earliest inspiration for world adventure. Eager to learn things and, above all, to discover the planet, I spent all my spare time after chores and homework — and for as long as parents and coal oil allowed — poring over the pages of the magazine's weekly presentations.

I was a dozen years down the path of my life when one particular issue took indubitable hold of my fancy. Its focus was Antarctica! Barely able to read the narrative (which I learned many years later was written by the National Geographic photographer Eliot Porter), it was more the fantastical panoramic black and white photographs that dominated my viewing, images that consistently held my attention at near-hypnosis interest levels, as I studied them day after day after day, until the pages became completely dogeared and the ink smudged by my fingertips. Yes, it was all about frozen snow and ice, both of which were of course indigenous to where I lived, but something about the infinite and desolate grays, and the mysterious shapes of ice looming within that landscape, captured and fascinated my imagination.

So it was that Antarctica left its permanent imprint upon my evolving mind. And with Dad's help, I even found it on the bottom of that twirling globe. Though still too young to know about airplane travel, I nonetheless figured out how I would get there. I would slide down to the Equator and then I would simply fall the rest of the way to the South Pole!

~ ~ ~ ~ ~ ~ ~

It is now 1976, about twenty-four years later.

One very early morning, a rugged-faced gentleman, all decked in soft-spoken manners and Northface gear, stepped into my small typing-service office in Santa Fe, New Mexico, carrying a large wooden cigar box containing thirty-six audio-cassette tapes which he asked me to transcribe and type into manuscript form — a slightly overwhelming and very arduous task given that this was way before the age and convenience of computers.

My receptionist had not yet arrived for front-desk duty, so I sat down with the gentleman to fill out the requisite forms and offer verbal estimates for his consideration. Pen in hand and face to the form, I asked: "May I have your name, please."

"Eliot Porter," the man said. My pen dropped, and for a few heartbeats, I lost my composure while my mind traveled with lightening speed back to that long ago *Life Magazine* bearing the images and stories of Antarctica, written and compiled by him.

I regrouped and, without too much obvious pause, though certainly with heightened curiosity, even a bit of hope, I asked:

"What is the subject of the tapes, if you don't mind telling me?"

Seeming to be a man of few words, he calmly offered no more information than: "They are the recordings of my last journey to Antarctica!"

An electric charge surged through me from top to bottom. I stopped writing, instantly, and taking a moment to look straight up at him, I dared to ask, rhetorically: "You are the Eliot Porter, whose *Life Magazine* photos about Antarctica I so thoroughly absorbed as a child long ago?"

"Yes, I am probably he." And he smiled ever so slightly, pleased, I think, to hear what I had just told him.

"What serendipitous connections life can bring!" I said. "Mr. Porter, I want you to know that those photographs left my hyper-imaginative child's mind with a genuine eagerness to travel and see the world, and even that part of the world. I have never forgotten those visually gripping ice images."

Proudly and confidently, he listened: "You will see it one day, and you will never forget the experience."

Countless hours and many days later, I completed the transcriptions. "What an unusual journey I have just vicariously enjoyed," I told a friend, "and with the added thrill of listening to Mr. Porter's voice tell the story!"

He came to retrieve his manuscript and pay his bill. He was very gracious and generous about all that, and then, with a handshake and a sincere hope that I would one day see this unbelievable part of the planet, he disappeared down the stairs and back to his home in rustic Tesuque.

~ ~ ~ ~ ~ ~ ~

About a year later, he stopped by once more, with his magnum opus now published. He gifted me with an uninscribed copy of the book, said thank you, and looking right at me, pulled a fifty-dollar bill out of his pocket and handed it to me, saying: "This is a downpayment for your journey to Antarctica! May it be your best adventure ever! Bon voyage!"

~ ~ ~ ~ ~ ~ ~

I received news fourteen years later, in 1990, that Eliot Porter had passed away. He was eighty-eight. Thanks entirely to him, the long ago images of Antarctica were now well reawakened; the idea of a some-day journey to this remote place began to take serious hold. With the passing of time and the consistent and coincidental occurrences of other related events, it became very clear to me: traveling to the antarctic would not just be another trip to take; it would be the earned journey of my lifetime, and Mr. Porter would surely be remembered during it and thanked for it.

~ ~ ~ ~ ~ ~ ~

On Halloween evening in 2009, amost another twenty years later, I was sitting at Café Flore in San Francisco's Castro neighborhood paging through the Bay Area Reporter. In it I saw a photograph in which I recognized my dear friend Tom, dressed in an elegant red velvet costume borrowed from San Francisco Opera's production of Puccini's *Manon Lescaut*. He and his partner Bill, both top-ranking concierges at the War Memorial Opera House, had for many years been involved in organizing sophisticated cruises around the world, which, I might add, they tried at least once a year for as many years to persuade me to join, unsuccessfully. Having now been disconnected from them during a huge personal transition, I took this photo as a sign that it was time to reconnect, and sent it to them along with my new address and phone number.

It wasn't two days before Bill telephoned to say, "Erika, what wonderful news! Now will you come on a cruise with us?" That was followed immediately by Tom sending via email a long list of cruise possibilities and details. There were seven or eight offerings to the usual destinations, but at the very bottom of that list, to my complete surprise, and I have to say, momentary apprehension, I read: 'Science/History Cruise to Antarctica'! My breath stopped. I studied what it said, re-read it, and then decided my excuse for not going would be the price — way out of range for my budget, and therefore out of the question, period.

~ ~ ~ ~ ~ ~ ~

Any number of days passed, and the thought of a cruise to Antarctica, a science/history cruise at that, would not leave me; it stuck like a bad bit of phlegm in my craw, until I woke up one morning feeling I could no longer procrastinate. I could no longer hesitate. Too many signs had pointed me in this direction. I finally bit the bullet, and, as if I needed a reason to justify the expense, I rationalized that it would be a great gift to me for my seventieth birthday! And, by dipping into my father's little inheritance, I would actually be bringing this story remarkably full-circle. With fear and daunting I signed up. The cruise was set for a year in advance, so plenty of time to prepare, to do research, to study . . . and even to cancel, if I got cold feet!

Over the next few weeks, while studying all the information, I was intrigued by a suggested reading list of three books. I smiled proudly realizing that for a number of years I had already had two of them, one of them, coincidentally, being Antarctica by Eliot Porter, whose entire original narrative I had of course transcribed so long ago.

~ ~ ~ ~ ~ ~ ~

And so, I took that long journey to the bottom of planet Earth, into the extensive waterways and channels surrounding the vast Antarctic Continent, an other-worldly place whose scope and size and breadth and depth seemed to have come into being from purest primordial nothingness.

Here is one episode from that unforgettable experience.

~ ~ ~ ~ ~ ~ ~

There are those who call Antarctica the sixth, even the fifth, continent. Since I was unable to find any official listings that substantiated which continents fell where in the numerical rank, I preferred calling it the seventh continent. There are seven of them and, coincidentally, seven is also one of my three favorite numbers. Regardless of its rank in the continental files, our cruise historians, in various lectures and presentations, reminded us constantly how Antarctica is the continent that has eluded man's understanding ever since it was officially sighted in the first quarter of the Nineteenth Century.

~ ~ ~ ~ ~ ~ ~

It was the middle of our voyage, and we were about to anchor in the center of a tiny volcanic island known as Deception Island, at the northern-most tip of the Antarctic Peninsula.

Very early on this frosty morning, I headed up to the outer deck, just in time to watch our brave seafaring vessel ease its way, very slowly and very dramatically, through a hazardously narrow passageway known as Neptune's Bellows, so named for the mythological Roman god and protector of people at sea. I wasn't sure whether to blame him, or give him credit, for our adventurous Captain's artfully intrepid maneuver through this two-hundred-and-fifty-meters-narrow gusty gateway, with its dangerous rock protrusion positioned far too precariously and far too few meters below the surface.

In a few minutes, we were securely anchored in a gargantuan caldera, upon an eight-kilometer-wide glassy lake inside this currently sleeping volcano. An estimated ten thousand years ago, according to scientists, an eruption blew the top off its towering mountain, ejecting enormous quantities of magma, then collapsing the chamber in a cataclysmic shudder, leaving its deep basin flooded by the waters of the antarctic's Southern Ocean. It is an active volcano, whose last blast occurred in 1970, and there is speculation among scientists it will erupt again in about ten more years as I write this, somewhere around 2020.

~ ~ ~ ~ ~ ~ ~

Once more, the mighty zodiacs and their trusty drivers delivered us safely to shore. After a short history briefing at the now defunct whaling station, a three-hour hike was planned to scale one of the higher ledges toward a glacier's edge, the top of which we could see from where we were presently standing, and from which, we were told, we would be able to look back and, for the first time, genuinely sense the immensity and vastness of the antarctic's watery expanse. Feeling enthusiastic about this particular adventure, I was eager to give it a try. By the expedition team's standards, this would be considered a medium difficult hike, due to the loose lava rock, and ultimately, the slippery, frozen snow at the foot of the glacier.

The bullhorn summoned and everyone began assembling in preparation for the hike, while Pieter, the Austrian meteorologist in the group, held our fascination with interesting tidbits. "Our ship from way up there will look like a mere toy in a pond," he said. "A perfect antarctic illusion of distance and height . . . and time. Because the atmosphere in Antarctica is so clear, one is easily deceived by distances. Mountains which seem fifty kilometers away may, in fact, be as far distant as two hundred kilometers."

Standing ready, in waiting mode, I was thinking how Deception Island seemed entirely other-worldly and that it felt very different from all other scattered rock-and-ice outcroppings we had so far seen throughout the Southern Oceans. For one thing, there was no animal life here. I could feel, with an enigmatic tug in my tummy, the vastness that Pieter had mentioned, the cold, black barrenness. Interested in all of it, I wondered where this adventure would take me.

By the time we began hiking up the side of the volcano, it had become a windless morning, not a breeze was stirring. A therefore bearable temperature was felt all around, and an eery tule fog was rising up out of the geothermal waters on the lake's edge. Reflecting from a lower ledge, enveloped by the comforting arms of this horseshoe-shaped island, I looked out to sea across the calm reservoir and beyond the narrow bellows; I couldn't help thinking of a poetic 'dämmerung' — the time of day when dusk begins to fall or dawn begins to break.

~ ~ ~ ~ ~ ~ ~

To deviate for a few paragraphs — at dinner the previous evening, I had had what I would call a rather elevated conversation with my favorite scientist, Randolph. The dialogue began with him asking an especially beautiful question: "So, Erika, what inspired you to visit Antarctica?"

I smiled. "Many things of course. To begin with, Antarctica has been on my radar since I was a very young girl; however, one of the more impalpable adult desires I brought with me was something I felt the mind or the senses might be almost incapable of experiencing or comprehending, given the relatively short span of this cruise."

Leaning one elbow on the table and facing me with some fascination, Randolph smiled and said: "That sounds very compelling!"

I took a deep breath and plucked up enough courage to elaborate my thought, trying not to sound too excessively eager: "What I would love to feel, and hear, is the silence; to be inside the silence beyond the silence — which I thought so much about at home while preparing my mind, heart, and soul, for this great Antarctic journey."

"Are you a poet?" he asked, bemused.

I shook my head in the positive. "I want to feel the inspiring power of a wild and pure landscape," I said. "I want to spend a few minutes in a place that will stir my creativity, endow my hopes, and spiritually connect me with the Universe surrounding me. A silent place that will make me listen even more deeply." I looked up and met his eyes briefly, reciting another part of the mantra I had been carrying in my inner pocket every day: "I want to be in the silence of strength, the silence of power, the silence of endurance, the silence of patience, the silence of waiting, and the silence of expectations. The overall silence that is so complete one begins to actually hear it."

Randolph, still smiling, wondered: "Are you willing to share what inspired all that in you?"

Another great question, I thought, and I told him: "During the Eighties I became very interested in and influenced by some of the writings of the American astrophysicist, Carl Sagan. His uniquely ethereal way of defining such moments in an almost transcendent language is what made this whole idea palpable for me."

"I think you will experience it, and I hope you do," Randolph said, with some empathy, and then he cautioned: "As you can guess, it can't be planned; but all you need to do is be observant and listen without anticipation or expectation!" I felt very reassured hearing that. I also felt a kindred spirit in Randolph, in that he knew what I was trying to say, having quite probably experienced such moments himself, being one of the few scientists on board who had made the lonely two-thousand kilometer slog all the way to the South Pole with a friend.

I went to my cabin that evening feeling tremendously elated — and hopeful.

~ ~ ~ ~ ~ ~ ~

The long trek about to begin, I positioned myself directly behind Randolph, who thankfully happened to be the leader for the group I was in that morning. Slowly we began snaking upward, a slightly steeper incline than I had suspected or hoped, if only because I had had some trepidations about vertigo in one other uphill hike, at Grytviken on South Georgia Island, so it was on my mind, but it was also in my best interests to give this climb a sincere attempt.

A short way up and along, I turned around for a brief second just to capture the visual of the endless line of red parkas inching along behind me, against an otherwise starkly white, gray, and black environment, and our ship, as predicted, completely dwarfed in the background amidst the tule fog. I gasped at the awe-inspiring sight, and I did feel a small twinge of dizziness just in that moment, but all still seemed fine. Along with the others, I continued to move upward and onward, inch by inch.

It was at about the halfway point, when I turned around once more, that a strange nausea hit me square in the pit of my stomach. I knew instantly I could not go on. "Randolph," I called out, with some embarrassment. He immediately stopped the line for a few minutes and turned around to check on me: "I think I'm falling; I'm feeling an unfamiliar dizziness, as if something is pulling me down."

He guided me downhill about thirty steps to a big boulder, and suggested: "Sit here, get your equilibrium re-set, you'll be fine. Try to stay until we come back, and I'll meet you here in half an hour." I complied, and was very happy the windless weather, though gray and overcast, was nice enough to allow me to just sit that long, without moving too much.

What an odd and disappointing sensation, I thought, feeling this strong interior force pulling me downward. But in not too long, I regained my bearings and footings and felt secure and comfortable enough sitting on that ancient and very solid rock.

And thus, without my realizing it, a most perfect experience inside a perfect moment had begun. The red-parka lines had completely disappeared behind the black lava-rock slope, and were on their way across a small valley to the foot of the glacier beyond. With everyone out of sight and sound, it was quickly sinking in that what was left of anything visibly human on the landscape, at this moment, for the next little while, was Me!

I was here, surrounded and enveloped by an exquisite whiteness overhead, in direct color opposite to the black volcanic lava; I was here, and completely alone.

To put a cosmic perspective on it, I had literally turned into one tiny, almost invisible, speck on this blue orb called planet Earth. Perched on one inconsequential fossilated boulder inside a colossal crater, in this commanding polar whiteness that is Antarctica, I was, in this instant, overpowered with feelings I could not fathom. I took a consummate and unbounded opportunity to retreat to my interior, to ruminate upon the smallness of man, and to ponder the immensity and abundance of the Universe.

I began thinking of my father and how very proud of me he would have been, and pleased. And in thinking about him just then, I remembered his enthusiasm while reading the profoundly stirring words of Carl Sagan, whose eloquent descriptions of extraterrestrial experiences, and their magnificence, grandeur, and scale, I thought might easily enhance my terrestrial experiences here just now, and make them seem even more tenuously delicate. I remembered Carl Sagan's words on the wall of my study in San Francisco: "It is overpowering to have a knowledge of the existence of something we cannot penetrate; perceptions, of the profoundest reason, and the most radiant beauty, which, only in their most primitive forms, are accessible to our minds: it is this knowledge and this emotion that constitute genuine adoration and divine venerableness."

~ ~ ~ ~ ~ ~ ~

And so, here, alone, in this mastodonic openness overlooking the sea beyond Neptune's Bellows for what seemed like hundreds of kilometers into endlessness, here, in this extreme stillness, I was experiencing my moment of silence. An utterly noiseless moment; finally, the silence beyond the silence.

All of this surprised me greatly, and I couldn't help smiling out loud at the affirmation that even silence was bigger and mightier than I was in this achromatic wilderness. I took off my parka-hood and beanie, and - just - listened. The longer and more intensely I listened, the more the silence grew. An ineffable and complete soundlessness! Not even the air crackled — as I remembered it from my youth in the frozen Northern Manitoba tundra. Sitting in this antarctic enormity, I could feel myself disappearing. Down below, I could almost hear the tule fog rising above the caldera. And looking beyond all that, way out into the distant and endless gray-ish white, I could only think of two words: infinite splendor. For these few minutes, probably the only few such minutes of my entire life, I had the privilege of feeling completely and happily alone on Earth, on the Great White Continent, on the edge of the planet, in an antarctic caldera, completely surrounded by a noiseless solitude. The only thing I eventually heard was the beat of my heart.

Incognizant of time passing, I had gone so far inside myself, and with such intensity, that I forgot, ever so briefly, where I was — and for just one anxious nano-second, I hoped I wouldn't be forgotten, left here to the whims of wintery weather and eventual fodder for feathered fiends.

Ultimately, it was a moment that I will cherish forever, a profound inner connection with the great Universe, as I comprehended it. I knew I would never again feel so distanced from anyone or anything while at the same time feeling completely bound to the planet itself, in a way that will remain indefinable for me for as long as I walk upon it.

For 'one brief silent moment,' I was in a place without buildings creaking, without electricity humming, without cars honking, without sirens screaming, and without people rushing.

I raised my head and had a small chat with Dad, who had decided just then, in his naturally conspicuous timing, to pass by in typical fashion and flare in that golden chariot he's been riding across the skies since the Summer of 2007. And then, with a sudden jolt, I was 'alerted' to the *sound* of a widespread pair of wings flying directly above me — a giant Wandering albatross floating across the airwaves. He was close enough to catch my eye looking up at him, like a guardian angel, a flying god: "Thank you for listening!" he seemed to say as he glided elegantly skyward and across the caldera's highest ledge out to the colorless gray sea.

~ ~ ~ ~ ~ ~ ~

That evening at dinner, back on board our muscular and robust ship, I sat happily at my small corner table, my back to the dining audience. In a mental trance, I gazed out of the big window, thinking about what had transpired on this day, when a gentle tap on my shoulder brought me back into the moment; it was Randolph. "May I join you?"

"Oh yes, please do." I was so happy to see him.

The sommelier poured some vintage wine into both our glasses, we toasted to life, he to his life-love Maggie and I to Michael in San Francisco, and then Randolph, with those wise eyes set deep inside his wizened and rugged face, stared at me, uttering a very slow but lyrical: "So . . . ?!"

That was all he needed to say. With those incessant tears forming in the corner of both my eyes, I said: "Randolph, dammit, you knew, didn't you? You knew this would be a moment for me!"

He smiled: "Well, let's just say, I felt this could be an advantageous time for you, and I was hoping on the way down the slope that you might have enjoyed, in part, what you came to Antarctica for."

Randolph was thrilled to hear my story, as we continued the conversation about wisdom and respect, ". . . two attributes one is obliged to apply," he admonished, "as I have learned after so many years of living within the antarctic environment." It was his sixteenth year, facing all the challenges, and he possessed the very calmness of spirit and purpose of life I so tried to keep nearest to me for the remainder of this voyage.

~ ~ ~ ~ ~ ~ ~

I wrote in my journal that night:

Finally I am speechless! I can not define the thrill of beholding the marvel and wonder of landscapes we often assume can only be seen on the lifeless moon. Though Antarctica may be similar in places to a lifeless moonscape, it is on our planet, and though hardly lifeless, it is one of the most soundless places I will ever have experienced.

~ ~ ~ ~ ~ ~ ~

Once home, I went straight to an old box of collected snippets and bits I had inherited from my father after his passing. I remembered, among the many scribbles and dog-eared pages, an old religious church calendar which he would have had no practical use for, basically, but upon whose blank backsides he had decided to make notes, about things he would hear on television, or read in books and newspapers — all of which, often and interestingly, were in that direct quagmire of paradox to the scriptural passages imprinted on the other side. By coincidence, it was on the back of the January (his birth month) calendar page where he had written: "Favorite words from genius people." It was there I found, carefully folded and preserved, and scotch-taped to the page, Carl Sagan's essay, "The Pale Blue Dot," inspired by the now-very-familiar photograph taken from outer space by Voyager 1 in 1977. The photograph was seen from six billion kilometers away, and planet Earth was a tiny bluish speck halfway down a dominating brown band of light within the darkness of deepest space. I understood perfectly why this had inspired Dad so much: ". . . our imagined self-importance, the delusion that we have some privileged position in the Universe, [is] challenged by this point of pale light. Our planet is a lonely speck in the great enveloping cosmic dark," Sagan had written.

It had the same effect on me.

Antarctica is strong because it is the ultimate natural 'unity'. It is the supreme vortex, the South Polar Axis, upon which the planet truly turns. It is the epitome of the human spirit being allowed to reach for the soul of man. It is a place where time recedes and life moves with its own rhythms. Gliding through this frozen world has been a profound revelation for me. In an earthen way of speaking, the experience has not created discomfort; it has only created gratitude for a privilege.

Antarctica is a musical apocalypse.

Antarctica is traveling to the very heart of ephemeral transience and home again.

His Antarctic Highness, Jackson, The King Penguin

SOUTH GEORGIA ISLAND, ANTARCTICA
January 2010

So far on and around South Georgia Island, the weather was being unusually cooperative. Which made the Captain very happy. Which made everyone happy, zodiac drivers, expedition leaders, and especially the guests. As well, the kindness of the weather gods provided the Captain, and Charles the team leader, an ideal but rare opportunity. In tandem, they quickly decided to ferry us from our temporary anchor at Stromness Cove around one more rocky corner to a rarely-seen but world-renowned location named Salisbury Plain, the entire Antarctic's most famous penguin colony — a rare gift to us and one that, due mostly to inclement weather conditions, many previous groups had sadly forfeited. Salisbury Plain is home to the world's largest gathering of the second-largest species of penguins, the Kings, not to be mistaken with the largest penguins, the well-known Emperors — which we would not be able to see since they lived nearer to the center of the continental ice shelf itself.

Salisbury Plain is also the main breeding ground in Antarctica for King penguins, their average population at this location estimated to be about two hundred thousand. As we neared the shore, this famous colony, beginning at the dark rocky landing beach and stretching literally as far as the eye could see, was easily visible from the ship's panoramic windows.

~ ~ ~ ~ ~ ~ ~

Filled with overwhelming excitement, I stepped out of the zodiac directly into what I would consider, for me, to be one of the most spectacular wildlife visuals in the animal world, a vision not only involving but truly overtaxing all the senses. Wherever I looked, all I could see was penguins, an enormous and endless forest of penguins, rising and stretching and swirling and weaving its way for several kilometers up the mountainside, all the way to the retreating glacier at the horizon. The braying sound was deafening and the viscous smell of the guano simply unbelievable. A completely unforgettable and undeniably potent first major penguin impression. Standing on the periphery, I was frozen in a solitary gaze at this overpowering scene and shaking my head in disbelief.

The lovely Maggie, a marine bio-scientist in the group whom I had already engaged in several conversations on this cruise, found me and came up to say: "Well, Erika, what do you think?"

"I don't know what to think, or even what to say. I'm speechless," I quipped, "probably for the only time ever in my life!" Maggie smiled.

"Is this the entire population of King penguins in the Antarctic?" I wanted to know.

"Not quite," she answered, "but it is the largest, and the reason most are on this particular shore which, end to end, stretches about five kilometers, is that the ocean here is full of krill."

~ ~ ~ ~ ~ ~ ~

One of the more enjoyable lectures for me had been presented by Maggie the previous day. A naturalist, she had spent many years studying the phenomenon of krill in these watery regions.

"At the bottom of the food chain of the Southern Oceans swims an extraordinary creature," she said. "It is the cornerstone species of the marine food web, not only the most abundant protein source, but the most important food source for the survival of the entire antarctic food chain. It is called the 'Kingdom of Krill', for the shrimp-like crustaceans that dominate and feed on phytoplankton, the unicellular algae free-floating in the antarctic waters. The tiniest of all sea creatures, only two centimeters long, it can live up to six years. There are estimated to be some six hundred trillion krill in the Southern Oceans, millions and millions of swarms of them, whose total weight in the seas constitutes from four to six billion tons. In perhaps better understood densities, that measures from ten thousand to thirty thousand individual creatures per cubic meter. Krill is the primary food for millions of fish, squid, seals, penguins, albatrosses, petrels, and the great Baleen whales. Without krill, the ecosystem of the Southern Oceans will collapse — a fear not taken lightly, in that about thirty-eight percent of the dry weight of krill is protein, and it is therefore exported to many countries and used for additives in vitamins for human consumption."

~ ~ ~ ~ ~ ~ ~

Breathless with anticipation, on my way into this forest of penguins, I followed close behind Maggie, plodding carefully across small, dangerously sharp rocks, into the midst of female Fur seal multitudes nursing their pups, and several hundred aggressive male Fur seals hissing at us without hesitation from their harems as we passed by.

Once beyond the furry mounds of seals, Maggie led me to a spot somewhere in the midst of all this profusion and I stopped, absolutely immobilized, thunderstruck, realizing I was suddenly surrounded by endless hectares of King penguins, feeling completely paralyzed inside a cacophony of symphonic sound that would have challenged any Twentieth Century twelve-tone composer. Still next to me, Maggie said: "And can you imagine; in the midst of all this discordance, penguin chicks are able to identify their very own parents' call in less than a few seconds!"

Maggie gave me permission to keep walking along to my heart's content. "Be calm," she cautioned, "they will come to you."

Daring to wander farther in and among them, I became almost tone deaf by their inharmonic trumpet calls. Non-stop and contagious, it was their way of ultimately arousing thousands to join in until their ecstatic and pompous display had spread throughout the entire colony. I pretended it was my welcome anthem! The whole situation was more than my overwhelmed mind could absorb or process in the short amount of time the group was allowed to remain here.

The visual beauty of the Kings, in stunning tailer-made coats of orange, yellow, black, and white, provided a veritable feast for the eye; three feet of noble distinction and grandeur standing out so exquisitely above the brownish carpet of thousands of chicks in their molting coats, interspersed and interwoven all throughout.

Numbed by their superior force and powerful nature, and literally being pulled inside their songs and throngs, the urge to just sit there a spell came easily. Time to be here, I thought, to observe their behavior, their actions and reactions, so humanlike, so fearless, and so friendly; to laugh at their humor and their physical antics, and to watch them feed their chicks and attend to them, and ultimately to watch them waddle through endless stagnant pools of mud and excrement as they headed in a single file line for a wash in the seaside surf below.

Once I had come to a good observation point, I also hoped for a non-guano-covered rock to sit on, but to no avail. In this universe, every square centimeter has penguin poop on it. Grabbing a few biodegradable tissues out of my pocket, I wiped what I could off the very top of one rock, and finally just sat down in my easy-to-clean waterproof pants, and focused.

My eyes were about to lock on one penguin, a tall guy, and very confident, when a gentle tap on my shoulder from my friend Tom brought the announcement: "That's Jackson!" Fair enough, I smiled, a good and full name for a handsome and strong penguin.

Completely upright before me, Jackson looked extremely dignified in his formal black and white coat, perfectly adorned by the orange patches extending downward on either side of his head and meeting beneath his chin like a starched collar, his outfit completed by his yellow bow tie mounted at the top of his silvery-white breast plumage.

Jackson liked me instantly. Docile, tractable, curious, and friendly, he stood tall on his patch, his heels in balance, and his back proudly arched. He did seem frozen to the ground, moving his regal head from side to side like a pivot upon his fixed body.

For a quiet moment, I wondered: am I mirroring him, or is he mimicking me?

Attempting several gentle movements and whispered sounds, I tried to take advantage of his laser-focused attention, in hopes of getting a specific reaction. He stared with keen interest, fixing his gaze on me, dead on, face to face, eyes unblinking. Finally, I opened my mouth to speak directly but softly to him. "Hey, Jackson," I said in a near whisper, and he responded, with a slight movement of his head.

Instantly excited by his reaction, I quietly said, "Oh, you are such a beauty", and this time he slowly blinked, closing and opening his eyes just once. How great! A phenomenal and astounding miracle moment.

I enjoyed this attention for a number of seconds, and then decided to test his focus on me. I leaned to my left and said, "Jackson, you are so handsome!" At the sound, his head turned right, and he blinked his eyes once more. I did the same thing the other direction — leaning my head to the right, saying "Jackson, you are very intelligent!" and he turned his head left, and acknowledged my compliment with another slow blink of his eye. I - was - elated, and felt I had opened a genuine and trusted communication channel with him.

Following that little experiment, Jackson and I both up-righted ourselves and stayed with the dead center, face to face, focus. He kept his diligent gaze completely locked on me, without even moving a feather — and without blinking! I was happy to remain in this stationary position for as long as he needed me there; in fact, I wanted to wait to see how long he would remain in the 'motionless silence' immediately surrounding him and me. I recognized how comfortable I was, just the two of us staring at one another. Had he been human, I might have felt different.

Lost in time, we kept watching one another for quite a while, at least for as long as it took me to wonder what might be going through his mind in these circumstances when, suddenly, he broke my train of thought and stepped a little closer toward me, leaving a distance between us of only about two feet —

that's not very far when you consider the size of this creature.

I took off my gloves and let my ungloved bare left hand dangle from my knee to see if his curiosity would entice him to come up and either peck it, or smell it, or . . . kiss it!! Within moments, he bent his elegant neck slightly downward directly toward my hand, and I felt his beak touch the top of it. Breathless, and filled with ethereal suspense, I waited for more contact. A tear fell and froze halfway down my cheek. He trusted me; in fact, he liked me, and I was unbelievably honored. I loved his concentrated gaze as I put the glove back on my very cold hand!

The silent dialogue went on a few minutes more, and then, perhaps feeling well enough acquainted, he released his feet from the heel position once more, moved just a few more inches closer, put on his emergency brake, and fixed his gaze upon me with full-on all-out intensity. How excruciating it was, knowing I wasn't allowed to just reach my arm around him to hug him! His body language gave me every clue that he was waiting for it. I could even read it in the bubble above his head!

Yes, I was beginning to feel a strong urge to put words in that bubble for him. Completely arrested by a sweet confidence in one another, and through my poetic mind, my imagination could hear him say: "Sometimes the sun sets only once a year where I'm from. I miss it when it's gone, and it seems that the night is prolonged until the sun rises again, thank goodness. It is so cold that my hips forget their dance and my feet have to keep crossing to keep their warmth; my lips even chap, and food completely loses its appeal. Thank you for understanding. I have enjoyed your visit very much."

For a few moments longer, I remained sitting there, wondering so many more things: what his age might be, what his story had been so far, how many handsome King penguins he had been responsible for adding to the population. I wondered if he remembered being a chick, like we humans remember being kids. I wanted to answer all his silent questions to me. I wanted to toss a little ping pong ball with him. I wanted to scratch his belly, swim with him, be wise like he was, to go home and forever live in peace and harmony in my world in the manner in which I had observed him living in his — the harshest environment known to mankind.

I also wondered how much eiderdown he had at the base of his perfectly groomed feathers to ward off severe temperatures in mid-antarctic winters. In his first lecture, Randolph, the ornithologist in the group, had explained about their perfect adaptation to extreme cold. "To keep warm," he had said, "penguins basically have four layers of feathers. The outer layers are very effectively insulated with down feathers. King penguins have about seventy down feathers per every square inch surrounding their entire body, right down to their feet."

~ ~ ~ ~ ~ ~ ~

I had a hundred more things to ask Jackson, and to discuss with him, tell him. But it was time to leave. We were being summoned back to our zodiac by the sound of our leader's bullhorn.

Oh, how I hated to leave, but slowly I got up to begin the departure. Jackson stayed in position, and I wondered if by now he might have become seriously frozen to the spot. He watched me very closely; I walked a few steps away from him and turned around just in time to watch him pry himself loose and follow me. "Where are you going?" he seemed to say, looking straight up at me as if he wanted me to stay forever.

"Oh Jackson, how I wish I could pick you up and carry you all the way to San Francisco!"

The urge to stroke and pet him was becoming more difficult to resist with each passing half-minute. I wanted to kidnap him and bring him home, and sadly, he provided no reason on Earth as to why that would be impossible to do. "Take me; what's so difficult about that?" he seemed to question.

I moved forward a few more steps, and still he followed, though leaving more and more distance between us. Ten more short steps away from him, and Jackson, in his perplexed stance, was still there watching me. I waved, and I could have sworn his flipper moved in response. I will say it did, because I know he wanted to!

Turning around one last time, I noticed, a few penguin steps away from Jackson, a chick, perhaps his own, edging toward him, still wearing its youthful plumage, which I called its brown Russian fur coat. Made me want to walk back over and fluff it nicely for him! And then, within moments, the chick's mother entered the fold. She must have just eaten a fish on her daily excursion into the sea, digested it slightly, and was now regurgitating the food into her chick's mouth. Standing by proudly, I could hear Jackson say, ever so acceptingly, if not submissively: "Living's not always easy, but you just have to make the best of it!"

Finally walking away from this unbelievable colony of King penguins, with a certain sadness and definite heaviness in my heart, I understood why the benevolent penguin is the one animal people love coming to Antarctica for.

~ ~ ~ ~ ~ ~ ~

While Salisbury Plain was, without doubt, the place to watch the most stately penguins on Earth, it was also an excellent area to observe the large Elephant seal, some males reaching the length of five meters and weighing up to five thousand kilos. I loved walking alongside the always informative Randolph. "How much time do they spend on land as compared to in the water?" I asked.

"Unbelievable as it seems, they spend about eighty percent of their life in the ocean," Randolph told me. "They are able to hold their breath for more than two hours, and they can dive down to two thousand feet deep, where they eat everything from skate and squid, to octopus, eel, and even small sharks."

~ ~ ~ ~ ~ ~ ~

Meanwhile, a katabatic wind was beginning its descent this mid-afternoon, howling its way down a glacier about a mile away. By this time in the cruise, we had become familiar with these seriously dangerous winds in the scheme of antarctic weather systems, and we knew we needed to act quickly when warned or called, or suffer worse than severe consequences.

Looking back to shore from the zodiac, I felt a big tinge of gratitude in my heart. To see all this and then, for a farewell reward, to look upward and hear the eery cries of two Light-Mantled Sooty albatrosses during their simulated in-the-air courtship flight, seemed the perfect epilogue to this day's fine and wonder-filled excursion.

~ ~ ~ ~ ~ ~ ~

Randolph, one of my favorite two of the scientists, gave another ornithological lecture on penguins later that day, now that we had seen the noble Kings and were heading into many more rookeries of various other kinds of penguins. "As you have already been told, King penguins are the second largest species in Antarctica," he said, "the Emperors being the largest, though regular travelers seldom see them as they live too many kilometers from here, toward the South Pole. King penguins, however, are the most attractive, and therefore also the most popular."

"Some of the facts about them are astonishing," Randolph went on. "For example, they dive deeper than any other penguin foraging for krill and other crustaceans. For breeding, they prefer flat coastal plains within easy reach of the ocean as their cycle is longer than that of any other penguins, chicks taking nearly a year to fledge. Kings do not lay the egg in a nest, but rather hold onto it on their feet, protecting it with a down-covered belly-wrinkle to keep it at the right temperature, for the entire fifty-five day incubation period, a period shared by both parents, each alternating with a shift lasting from six to eighteen days. The non-breeding parent goes to sea for long foraging trips while the breeding parent patiently holds the egg, awaiting the partner's return."

"When the chick hatches, it likewise spends the first thirty days on the feet of its parents. Then," Randolph went on to explain, "the chick is delivered to a crêche (a group) with other chicks while both parents go to sea for extended periods. It is common for these chicks to lose half their body weight during this time, from both stress and loneliness, because they have no food while waiting for their parents to return with it."

I raised my hand to ask: "To what age do mature King penguins live?"

"King penguins can live to over thirty years and they always return to their same site to breed," he said.

I was pleased to know this, relieved actually, because it meant that perhaps someone, from somewhere on this planet, might return here again one day and have another visit with my friend Jackson. Possessive of considerable wisdom along with a great sense of humor, he would have exhorted the onlooker: "Please, when you see Erika from San Francisco, give her my love, and tell her I think she lost her heart in Antarctica!"

~ ~ ~ ~ ~ ~ ~

Late in the evening, hiding away in the ship's little library, I wrote in my personal journal:

This day I have been privileged to wander among the most distinctively handsome feathered creatures on Earth, the King penguins. It has been magical for me. Even in the middle of thousands of them, surrounded by guano excrement everywhere — the strongest smell ever to hit my nose! — interspersed with several dead penguin carcasses here and there, eagerly waiting to be snatched up for lunch by a few bellicose petrels flying overhead, and the braying louder than I could have imagined, it was impossible not to feel a sense of awe, to feel a fundamental identity with their almost-human aspect. Their awkward gait on land, their heroic determination to survive in the most inhospitable place on Earth, are only two of the many characteristics that endear them. It is difficult not to fall in love with penguins; I have just crawled around in one of the noisiest, slimiest, smelliest rookeries of the antarctic regions, and though I arrived back on the ship, perhaps a little hard of hearing or unable to get the viscous scent out of my nose, I will forever remember the dignity of this creature, and its comical, almost human, bearing. Penguins are a constant source of inspiration.

~ ~ ~ ~ ~ ~ ~

Jackson taught me more than I could ever have bargained for, all within the few minutes in which he allowed me to enter his world, where I was able to realize his approach to life, his patience, his heartful understanding of, albeit, featherless creatures standing before him. Within the mass of Salisbury Plain, he was such an important part of one of the most amazing nations on this planet.

VI.
WAIT, SOMETHING
HAPPENED

It's A Long Way To Reykjavik . . .

REYKJAVIK, ICELAND
July 1968

. . . especially dressed in a nightgown!

And to make matters even more exciting, I was on the first journey of my lifetime to Europe.

It was the Summer of 1968 and I was living way down south on the Gulf of Mexico. I had set up house in the beautiful seaside town of Corpus Christi, in a small dilapidated one-bedroom apartment, the upstairs of a somewhat neglected duplex. That was not so interesting, but I lived across from a lovely little park, in which stood a one-hundred year old wood and adobe structure, the home at that time of the town's small but thriving one-room art museum. There I worked as the happy receptionist. The art director, Cathleen, was a classy southern belle, a daughter of the American Old South. Her every day entrance through the front door of the museum brought a big rainbow into my otherwise still vulnerable and mostly unformed daily life.

A year inside the wondrous world of visual art had begun to leave me with an extreme eagerness to visit the great museums of Europe, if not a desire to test my independence into the adventure. I took courage and, with Cathleen's urging and inspiration, booked my first flight to Europe. I would fly on Braniff Airlines to New York, and from there, I had the choice of either continuing with Braniff across the Atlantic to London, or to do something exotic like fly on Icelandic Airlines to Reykjavik in Iceland, and proceed from there to Luxembourg City in the Benelux countries. Then I would travel by train to Germany, along the historic Rhine River to Cologne, where I could begin visiting some of the many museums and art galleries.

The whole scenario sounded like a lot of first-time fun, so I purchased my ticket, and left for three weeks.

The Braniff airplane landed at Kennedy Airport, and I was thrilled speechless. All these wonderful firsts I was beginning to pile up in my life, taking charge of me, by myself, for myself.

Kennedy Airport was to be a three-hour stopover, but the Icelandic Airlines connecting flight didn't happen. About one hundred of us were waiting at the boarding gate when the announcement came that the plane had mechanical issues and we would consequently not be departing until early next morning. It was a slightly disorganized and confused cattle stampede, though no less exciting, as they loaded us onto a shuttle bus that took us to a B-class hotel on the periphery of the airport. My assigned room happened to be one floor above the entrance, which could, I thought, either be advantageous or not, depending on what circumstances lay ahead. Noisy it was, without a doubt.

So far, I was thrilled with the mis-adventure. Not bad, from my perspective, never having been anywhere or done anything like this before. The only thing not so interesting for me was a voucher for a meat and potatoes dinner in the dining room buffet. No classy lounges or high-end bars where one could while away an evening with oysters on the half-shell and chilled white wine. So I passed on the buffet, and went instead to a small general store boutique on the ground floor where I found some crackers and half liter bottles of red table wine. Not being able to afford anything better, I got one of each and took them up to my room, where I officially commenced a new chapter in my life, the early writings of my first genuine world travel journal while sipping on wine out of a plastic bathroom cup.

I was enchanted.

Eventually, I got into my long cotton nightgown and before pulling the shutters for the night, I rang the concierge to ask that he please wake me at a certain hour as a shuttle was coming by very early in the morning to take us back to Kennedy Airport.

I fell asleep smiling with pride and thinking with joy about my debut landing in Europe next day.

~ ~ ~ ~ ~ ~ ~

Early next morning, I was suddenly awakened, not by the concierge as arranged, but by the noise of people traffic and horns honking loudly and incessantly below the window of my room. I bounced out of bed, pulled aside the brocaded curtains, and peered down through the shutters to see busses approaching to . . . um . . . Wait a minute, that was the shuttle bus that was taking our group back to the airport! I recognized some of the people from the day before, climbing aboard with suitcases in hand. It was then I realized in a complete panic the concierge had forgotten to ring my room. I tried to ring the front desk, but apparently there was unusual chaos in the lobby, so no one answered. In a momentary state of bewilderment, I froze.

Fortunately, I had laid my travel clothes neatly on top of the suitcase next to my bed so I could hop out of bed in the morning, brush my teeth, and be downstairs in good time. There wasn't time to do anything but put my all-weather coat on over my nightgown, making sure it was buttoned all the way, slide into my walking shoes, and head down there. Suitcase in hand, along with a shopping bag containing my intended travel clothes, a skirt and a sweater, I ran down the stairs and out the door somewhat disheveled, somewhat dismayed, and very confused. The bus driver was still there, waiting for stragglers I assumed, and I climbed aboard, noticing the bus almost full of passengers, all neatly dressed and faces washed and hair in place! I plopped down in the first empty seat I saw, near the front of the bus, next to a young man, and heaved a sigh of relief, though feeling not at all in possession of my mental faculties. I was very uneasy and embarrassed, wondering if anyone would notice I was inappropriately dressed.

"Are you okay? Where are you going?" the young man next to me asked.

"I'm not really okay, and I'm hopefully on my way to Reykjavik!" I burst forth, in a very perfunctory manner.

A few minutes later, one more confused passenger came on board, looking about as bewildered as I was. She, however, seemed fully dressed, and I thought to myself, had I responded calmly instead of reacted in a hurry, I could probably have done the same. But this being my first journey of this magnitude, I had no idea how to judge time under any circumstances.

The driver started up the bus and we were shuffled back to the airport to the Icelandic Airlines terminal. Like a fearful kid on its first day of school, I was overwhelmed and disoriented in a crowded airport, and feeling as if everyone was staring at me since I was only half dressed. A service person on the floor could see the perplexed look on my face, and kindly guided me to the line for check-in. By some miraculous intervention, I found myself directly ahead of the same young man who had been next to me on the bus.

My turn came in the check-in line, and proudly I showed my new and shiny passport to the flight assistant, handed over my suitcase to check through to Luxembourg City, and got my seat assignment, next to the window of course — a must for novice travelers, as far as I was concerned! "See you on board," the young man behind me said, with absolute nonchalance.

We boarded, and my shopping bag and I got safely buckled in for my first partial trans-Atlantic journey, a six-hour flight to Iceland. Not too long after settling in, the same young gentleman came into view once more, and voilà, sat down right next to me. "Do you mind?" he quipped. "I asked if the seat next to you was available since I am traveling alone as well."

I really had no feelings one way or another. Exhausted from all the nervous upheaval, I fell asleep as soon as the plane was airborne, remembering just briefly the exhilaration of take off itself. At some point I woke up and thought about getting into my street clothes. However, I quickly gave up that idea, seeing that the lines to the only two toilet facilities were endless. The women's restroom in Reykjavik's airport, where we were scheduled for a three-hour layover, would serve my purposes well enough.

In the meantime, there was another first to enjoy: the staggering views out of my window as we flew over the fjords and mountains of southern Greenland, and the giant greenish-white icebergs floating in the sea directly beneath us. It seemed incredible to realize that what floats above the water is only the tip of these giant icebergs.

Eventually, a small meal was served, which gave the young man next to me his opportunity to engage in some chat. "I'm Willem," he said, "from Berlin. May I ask where you are from?" How polite, I thought, and I gave him my name, and a few other details. He went on to tell me he had just spent six months in New York City as an apprenticed art student. I thoroughly enjoyed hearing his story, and with considerable envy. It was all about the big worldly adventure of meeting people from all kinds of fascinating places for all kinds of fascinating reasons. It struck me that he was quite a bit younger than I was and already having these grand experiences.

In a few hours, the captain announced we were landing. My happy heart was racing with excitement realizing I had just made my first partial crossing over the Atlantic on my way to Europe, and as a bonus, I was about to set foot on Iceland.

Emerging from the restroom with my street clothing in place at last, and my confidence back intact, I found a savory-smelling bistrôt and sat down to read the small lunch menu: a crisp rye cracker spread with yoghurt, pickled herring, and sprinkled with toasted seaweed proved an interesting temptation. Together with a very sweet apple cider, which I also saw on the menu card, this was a good first taste into foods of other lands.

Shortly we were called to re-board and I was filled with sudden excitement; only halfway to Europe at this juncture, but so pleased with the entire adventure so far, mishaps and all. Back in my seat once more, I smiled to myself. I felt like I had been on a movie set these first twenty-four hours! It's always about impressions on a first journey anywhere. In all, today was not a bad beginning. And I would have a unique story to tell some day!

The Plaka In Oaxaca

OAXACA, MEXICO
December 1997

Several months before the December/January holiday season, I had given myself two choices for travel destinations: I could either go to the frozen semi-tundra of Manitoba in central Canada and be with my beautiful parents for a traditional family Christmas, in Winter temperatures of anywhere from forty-five degrees below zero, without the windchill factor, or I could go the opposite direction, to the mid-December jungle heat of Oaxaca in South Mexico, with temperatures well into the nineties, alongside high humidity. Truthfully speaking, neither was fully appealing to me, but, sorry, Mom and Dad, I chose southern warmth over northern chill. Just before Christmas, I left for Oaxaca, the Mexican state next to Chiapas bordering on Guatemala in Central America.

A chaotic arrival at Mexico City's almost impenetrable airport, but a decently expeditious transfer from one flight to another, landed me safely in Oaxaca City's much smaller and far less contentious airport.

Eager to get to the little hacienda I had rented in Oaxaca City, I hurried out of the airport, and headlong into the middle of rancid humidity. No surprise, given the curbside bustling with what seemed to be dozens of displaced families — moms, dads, children of all ages, hoping to get somewhere, waiting for something, waiting for someone, for a home, for a life!

A non-air-conditioned taxi crammed full of me and three other overheated and sweating passengers barreled into town, and dropped us off at our respective places. I was thrilled to step out of the taxi and come immediately face to face with the beautiful villa once owned by Hernán Cortés, a Spanish conquistador who, in the early Sixteenth Century, had become the First Marquis of the Valley of Oaxaca. The villa was on the appropriately-named bulevar Cinqo de Mayo, and the little carriage house I had rented was directly behind the main building — an enchanting two-room adobe structure with lofty ceilings and arched doorways, situated next to a flourishing garden. I could see myself enjoying mornings sitting next to the oval-shaped pond with floating blue morning glories, drinking delicious Mexican coffee, and writing a few thoughts into my daily journal.

~ ~ ~ ~ ~ ~ ~

I had arrived close to midnight, but was in no frame of mind for sleep. A walk to the square, just a few blocks ahead, sounded very appealing. The night was balmy and wonderful; the air felt alive with celebratory people noises, and I wanted to join in. It was Christmastime, after all, and this seemed like a great place for such colorful festivities.

Following the people sounds brought me directly to the heartbeat of Oaxaca City's center, the zokalo — a moving kaleidoscope of vibrance and color! My little guidebook had actually defined this square as one of the most beautiful in all of Mexico. I stood off to one side and watched. Everywhere, families were gathered in three generations around outdoor café tables, talking, eating, singing, playing flutes and guitars and accordions, and everyone doing a dance of some kind. Happy little ragamuffins on curbsides begging, pretty little girls in white dresses and bare feet swirling about like angels. Moms and dads with babies, young children, and dogs, walking through. Bunches of multi-colored balloons being hawked to the revelers sitting around the square. A showcase of activities more variegated than an artist's impressionist canvas.

Most importantly, this was a scene to remember.

Looking upward, I noticed people leaning over the edge of several rooftop café bars atop one-story buildings around three sides of the square. This had my curiosity piqued, so before wandering back to the hacienda, I went looking for a stairway to one of these enchanting places, and walked into a winebar called Frieda's, as in Kahlo. One could sit at a table, enjoy a chilled beer or a cooled Chilean wine, and watch the activities of the entire square from up there. Added to the twilight ambience was a groovy little jazz band, much to my delight and joyous completion. And as if all that wasn't enough, I fell in love with Sandor, the delightful and charming bartender.

Sandor welcomed me to Oaxaca City, and stood by while I asked questions about what kind of wines they had. He confessed their choice was limited, but then he said: "Madame, tell me what you would like, and I will find it for you!" Immediately, I knew that if he didn't have it here at the bar, he would in all likelihood go somewhere and get it.

So, I said, "How about a Chilean sauvignon blanc?"

Without hesitation, Sandor excused himself, promising to be right back, and within ten or so minutes, he appeared with a bottle of white wine. "My friend is the sommelier at a nice restaurant near the zokalo," he said, "and he carries many fine wines."

What a captivating introduction to this fabulous place on my first night out. Sandor poured me a glass, and for an hour or so I sipped with pleasure on this delicious elixir vitae, relishing every minute of being here, listening to every satin note of the jazz combo until my wine glass was empty. I paid my bill, tipped Sandor nicely, and said I'd be back the next evening. Smiling out loud, he promised to keep the bottle of wine for me.

Strolling back to my little cabaña, feeling quite euphoric, I couldn't wait for the remainder of the night to pass so I could get back in the morning and discover more of this place whose exuberance had bewitched me in one evening.

~ ~ ~ ~ ~ ~ ~

Next day's breakfast by the morning glory pond was a pure delight. Fresh fruits, artfully arranged on a colorful ceramic plate and crisp sopapillas in a little woven basket with sage honey on the side would satisfy anyone's palate. A cup of robust Mexican coffee rounded things out nicely and I felt primed for the day. A few thoughts needed to be entered into my journal, and then it was time to amble back to the square.

The entire town was teeming with colorful people, special events, and seasonal festivities. A proliferation of bazaars, reminiscent of Istanbul's own, had somehow sprouted overnight, already selling everything imaginable, from special crafts and decorations of the season to special dessert tostados heaped with colored creams and shredded coconut. Even hair salons were in on the action, their front-of-shop sandwich boards displaying exquisitely hand-drawn watercolor renderings of holiday hair fashions.

Walking through, I felt buoyed by the spirited liveliness of these enthusiastic people, their endless reasons for celebration, and their kind and compassionate exchanges with visitors.

On the fourth side of the square, an extension of the area led to one side of the city's Cathedral, whose exterior wall facing the zokalo had been decorated with multi strings of live flowers, mostly white chrysanthemums, zigzagging up and down and sideways across its entire surface. And against a terra cotta fence on the plaza in front of the Cathedral, enormous piles of newly broken pottery shards, an end-of-year tradition that was to bring good luck: shedding old habits, and beginning a new chapter, as one person, a tourist who had visited Oaxaca City numerous times, put it. I stepped inside the Cathedral for a few minutes, and there, in all its bright-colored finery, was the Natividad Familia, blown-up balloons hanging above it and blue plastic flowers strung all around it, in preparation for Christmas Eve mass.

Filled with enough visions of color and wonder for now, I went back to the square to sit down under the covered arcades and sip on a chocolate espresso while I watched the natives traverse. Straight ahead, an ancient tree — a two-thousand-year-old acacia, I was told — created a perfect umbrella across the zokalo, and a peaceful cover under which the townspeople could meet on any evening. A soft breeze wafted through and I was very satisfied.

~ ~ ~ ~ ~ ~ ~

One reason for traveling to Oaxaca was to visit the partially excavated Mixtec-Zapotec ruins of Monte Albán. One of the earliest abandoned cities of Mesoamerica (a pre-Sixteenth Century area extending from Central Mexico to Costa Rica), Monte Albán had been the pre-eminent Zapotec socio-political and economic center for nearly one thousand years. Its restoration at this point was still on-going.

Getting there was an unforgettable adventure. A vehicle the locals called a truck bus, a handmade reconstruction, I swear, of parts and bits from various old trucks and buses, and much too dilapidated for my comfort level, picked up a small group of us at a prescribed corner near the square. One farmer was already on board in the bus-top fenced in space, with a very small goat and several chickens in a cage.

The journey began, and I was, quite frankly, frightened. I had been on many mountainous roads in other parts of the world before, not to mention in questionable vehicles, but this trek was the scariest ever for me. Though it only needed to travel about ten kilometers, and climb about sixty-five hundred feet to the top, it moaned and groaned and squealed non-stop, especially around several unnerving hairpin turns without guardrails on the side for protection. Of course, once at the top, the breathtaking scene was well worth the death-defying ride.

I wandered off, immediately, to the largest and highest temple of the maze, entering it and climbing up through it to the top, where I found a flat surface to sit on, from which I could absorb the perfect 360 degree view, think about the civilization that built this place of phenomenal magnitude, and ponder the power that dominated it for several centuries.

~ ~ ~ ~ ~ ~ ~

I sat there a while, gazing out across the large expanse of this shaved-off mountain top and its many structures. Sipping on delicious water from my plastic bottle, I was enjoying the calm, and the good fortune of being comfortably removed from the daily barrage of interruptions from students and faculty at the university, when I felt a tap on my shoulder. "Erika?" the voice said. I was not imagining this. In shock, I turned around, wondering who on earth had found me here. "Hi", the young man said. "Do you remember me? I am Robert; I was a student in the Theatre Arts Department about five years ago."

In total disbelief, especially since I had just been thinking what a relief it was not to be interrupted by anyone, I raised myself off the rock seat, shook myself out of my seance, to acknowledge this . . . Robert. "Forgive me, but tell me what I would remember you for!" That was always my best segue into the situation, as there were so many stellar performances by incredible acting students in various productions, and sadly I could not remember them all, but little by little I had Robert coming back into my radar, or at least pretending to.

We chatted a while, Robert telling me that he had met an anthropology student several years ago, and they hooked up and decided to literally dig their way through Mexico and Central America, as they visited well over one hundred anthropological sites, made notes, and in general lived under the stars, in love, and as if there would never be a tomorrow.

Fully mentally muddled by this little encounter, I nonetheless told Robert I was thrilled they said hello, and if they were crossing through Oaxaca City, to stop by the square on a certain night, and they would find me enjoying an evening of wine and jazz, under the same stars, and in the always convivial spirit of Latin America.

~ ~ ~ ~ ~ ~ ~

The creaky vehicle with iffy brakes and an overheated clutch managed to deliver a group of us safely back to the city square. I went home to have a short siesta and then shifted gears for another evening in my secret hideaway, Frieda's Winebar atop the zokalo, with white chilled wine waiting for me and an exotic jazz band playing the sweetest melodies.

Sandor had seen me approaching. By the time I climbed up the stairs and found 'my' table, he had already poured a cool glass of my Chilean wine, and next to it placed a little plate of three skewers of the most delicious pickled olives I had ever tasted.

"Sandor, I have never seen olives served on a skewer. What is the process?"

He was thrilled to tell me: "We take the pits out of the olives, then put about five on a skewer and stand them up in a big jar filled with olive oil, seasonings, and a lot of tequila!" He laughed out loud telling me about this concoction. They were delicious! I had never had tequila-pickled olives.

Needless to say, I needed no dinner after those fabulous little tapas. I wandered home very happy and very ready for some good sleep. I was feeling very nostalgic, remembering fun family Christmases of years gone by. Everything today had been a collectively wonderful experience, a richly rewarding combination. I wanted to shout and dance, and wrap myself in the warm pleasures of this intoxicating city.

~ ~ ~ ~ ~ ~ ~

Another important and well-preserved group of ruins I wanted to visit made up an entire village called Mitla — on the flat this time, about thirty-five kilometers distant from the square of Oaxaca City. According to research I had done, some of its sites had been perpetuated for ten thousand years, and I wanted to spend some time in this quaint place with its elaborate mosaics, and its intricate and geometric fretwork panels covering entire walls and façades of buildings. Mitla was also noted for extravagant tombs and sophisticated underground passages, many of them lined with chacmools, the tigers carved from various colors of marble.

I went to the square to try to roust a taxi. The third one finally agreed, but with some reluctance. Leaning toward his car window, I understood him to say something about "Chiapas, peligroso, asesinatos . . . !" and realized it was probably in reference to a ruthless massacre that had occurred there a few days ago, on December 22nd.

Chiapas was the next state over. Several heavily armed men in dark police uniform had stormed a small village church and, in a bloody shooting spree, killed about fifty women and children who had been kneeling in prayer. I had caught the incident on television news in the foyer of the hacienda where I was staying, where several of the service people had gathered and were, with considerable fear in their eyes, watching the event being replayed over and over. I remember feeling a pall as I walked through, but didn't otherwise place too much immediate relevance on the situation since I didn't really have a proper perspective in terms of the distance between here and there.

The taxi consented, and we agreed on a fair price for the trip, there and back. We had gone a few kilometers out of the city, when I began to notice, with some anxiety, armed military soldiers placed sporadically but very strategically behind sandbags all along this dusty car path they called a road. The taxi driver kept driving, quietly, looking left and right, not showing too much disquiet, and I tried not to reveal my apprehensions.

When we arrived in Mitla, I paid the driver double the fare, gave him the understanding I would only be about an hour, and he gave me the assurance he would wait for me. As I literally ran through various ruins, tombs, and village buildings, I was disappointed at having to rush, but I also sensed a restlessness. Unfortunately, my mind was preoccupied with imminent danger, and I was not able to enjoy the visit as much as I had planned to. A couple, tourists from New York I found out, were also there, and we fell into a short conversation about the whole situation. They had been there for a few hours and were, themselves, becoming a little apprehensive. I told them they were welcome to join me for the return in my hired taxi, which they were extremely grateful for. My sweet driver was, indeed, patiently waiting for us in the same spot where he had dropped me earlier, and we got in for the drive back. He didn't mind two more passengers, and they paid him well when we finally arrived back at the square in Oaxaca City, filled with relief but also caution. There was definitely and suddenly an agitated feeling in the air. The always lively square seemed caught in a mysterious hush.

Walking back to my cottage, I noticed police vans unloading young men on various street corners, apparently armed soldiers but not in uniform. They seemed to be carrying their loaded guns as if they knew exactly what to do with them, and I suddenly began feeling uneasy. My general inclination was to try to not worry too much, though the situation became entirely too unnerving when I realized they really were everywhere.

A sad disruption. The spirited festivities of a few days ago had been dimmed considerably, but people seemed to stay quietly put and carry on with the activity of the moment. I kept walking, and made it back to the hacienda, where by now about twenty or so service people were nervously huddling in the foyer, talking in low voices, all looking rather worried, but still making the effort to smile at me as I walked through. I had a bottle of wine delivered to my room from the service kitchen, from which I had two glasses, to numb the fear a little, and hopefully help me take a short nap.

Close to midnight of my last evening, I wanted to walk back to the zokalo to Frieda's and see what was going on. The streets seemed still and peaceful, and I saw no soldiers or police anywhere just then. All was eerily serene, like the calm before a storm. I walked by the Cathedral, and I could hear the angelic voices of children singing at a late mass. Beautiful balm for my nerves, which were beginning to tingle ever so slightly.

I crawled up to Frieda's, and there was Sandor, watching the news. He came over to my table and said: "Madame, no worries, no worries. Que está bien!" Coming from him, I felt assured, and in a few minutes, he had a glass of chilled wine set before me, this time accompanied by twice as many tequila-pickled olives on sticks, at no extra charge.

~ ~ ~ ~ ~ ~ ~

I had my journal with me, and tried to write a few feelings and thoughts:

Everyone is very very subdued. The celebratory mood has definitely subsided. Sandor has come to sit at my table, and I have invited him to pour himself a glass of the Chilean sauvignon blanc. People are beginning to leave the café, and soon it is just him and me, with one million stars in the night sky above us.

I sense an underlying and irretrievable loss among the local people; they seem to be keenly aware of on-going bloody battles between their Catholic religious activities and warring Mexican government factions. Such mysterious conundrums as they try in deepest devotion to their religion to enjoy festivities, regardless.

~ ~ ~ ~ ~ ~ ~

Being a wonderful gentleman, Sandor walked me home to the hacienda that evening, and gave me a hug at the gate. We shook hands, after which he turned around to leave, saying: "Adiós, hasta mañana!" And I didn't have the heart to tell him I would not be back. I was scheduled to depart from Oaxaca City the following morning.

~ ~ ~ ~ ~ ~ ~

I did not sleep well that night. Feeling somewhat uneasy and flustered from the events of these last few days, I got up, packed my bag, had a bit of fruit and coffee for breakfast by the morning glory pond, and wondered just how this day would actually progress. I checked out, exchanging all sorts of pleasantries with the concierge and the rest of the staff, and then waited for my taxi.

As it turned out, it was a fortuitous move to allow myself two hours of time to get the relatively short distance to the airport. And all was fine — until we got to the outskirts of the city, just at the turn-off to the airport. Somewhere within the early hours of that morning, Oaxaca City had been completely barricaded and surrounded by soldiers at regularly placed intervals, each armed with a two-foot long machete. As well, a few men in the lineup had guns, presumably loaded. Dilapidated vehicles had been randomly lined up, and huge rocks and junk metal out of ditches scattered between. Traffic had come to a standstill and could not move in either direction. The airport was another fifteen kilometers or so down the highway. I could see taxis stranded for the same reason on the other side of the barricade.

My driver halted, didn't say a word, and I was in the back seat sweating bullets. I had never seen such bleak, dismal, and downright menacing people, lined up as far as the eye could see, each one with a blade in his hands. A convulsive shiver ran through me, and I couldn't help thinking the Zapatista warlords would take great pride in telling these young men to go out and chop up a few people so they could qualify for the army!

I had never been in such a predicament before. I would definitely call this a do or die situation, and I was not about to die. I decided to ignore imminent danger, and take my chance at getting across the barricade. Bodily and boldly I stepped out of the taxi. "Tener cuidado!" the driver offered. "Be careful," as

I inched cautiously forward. In doing so, I cautiously locked eyes with the nearest soldier and mouthed: "Aeroport . . . !" He said nothing, of course, only stared back with skeptical eyes. Remaining completely focused on him, my mind kept repeating with unbelievable swiftness: "Let me go, set me free, please don't kill me," and then some kind of adrenalin took over. I took my chance and crossed the barricade between two bent and twisted sheets of rusty metal, and kept walking with a confident pace, trying not to run, as that might make him suspicious. Once across, my knees completely wobbly and my mind in some kind of overdrive, I felt as if any minute I would be shot in the back, or stabbed by a machete.

Taking a deep breath and feeling successful so far, I crawled into the nearest taxi, which had another passenger already inside, trying to get into the city. A very nice driver turned around to me and pointing to the other passenger motioned that we were going to drive a ways around the periphery of the barricade to drop him off and then we would go back to the airport. Eternity is not something that can be measured, but these next minutes were definitely a very long eternity. Due to all the obstruction, it was necessary for the driver to make some unusually long detours, but he managed, after all was said and delivered, to get me to the airport on time. With an enormous sigh of relief, I more or less bolted into the airport building on one side, and out the other, to catch my flight to Mexico City. The plane was literally half empty, and I realized there must have been people still trying to cross that same barricade.

A rattled and disconcerting departure, to say the least. The plane took off, and I slumped into my seat. Feeling mentally wrecked and physically not only a little immobilized, I kept thinking back to the beauty of this country and its sweet people, juxtaposed against a despicable army of police for whom the only thing important in life seemed to be carrying weapons to threaten and destroy all that.

~ ~ ~ ~ ~ ~ ~

Flying home, I was vividly remembering some poignant images that I knew would remain permanently inscribed upon my mind, not least of which would be this morning's escape itself from beautiful downtown Oaxaca City.

I would always remember the little boy leaning against a pecan tree in the park across bulevar Cinqo de Mayo, playing sad and simpering melodies on an accordion almost as big as he was, staring at me with huge purple plum eyes as I passed by at twilight.

There was the demure young chambermaid at the hacienda, who became the daily beneficiary of the chocolates brought with every morning's coffee to the pond-side.

I would never forget the little girl on a smoggy street corner with noisy traffic, her nose covered for protection against fumes, as she worked her American hot-dog stand, with little concern about the same fumes infecting the food she was serving!

And how could I not remember the elderly beggar lady on the zokalo, shuffling about with her cane and a permanent smile on her hollow face, collecting empty beer and soda cans, stuffing them slowly and methodically into her various plastic and cloth bags.

There were those proud village women, plumed with handsome dignity and plenty of assurance, sandals of old tires under their feet, and, upon their backs, wearing their infants like future potentates, as they stepped into the Cathedral for daily prayers.

I had seen so much graffiti everywhere on old brick and mortar city walls, and myriad slogans with baffling permutations of political initials, red paint dripping down in frenzied blobs from their mostly violent exhortations.

These are indeed some of the imprints that have remained with me, mixed with a profusion of somber nobility, fierce pride, undeniable patience, and gentle caring, as I remember their consistent pace, onward, forward, toward the next song, the next soda can, the next scene, the next state of chaotic affairs.

A country known for coups and revolutions; for submissions and celebrations.

How sad, how beautiful, how true.

Cries from the soul, raw with pain, and sometimes ugly in honesty.

The Round Table in a Paris Corner

PARIS, FRANCE
Spring 1999

I have journeyed to Paris countless times. Each time is different, introspectively and contemplatively; each time teaches me to appreciate anew the elemental spontaneity of life within the singularly unique milieu that is Paris.

And so it was. Strolling one evening at dusk across the Seine to the Left Bank, I chanced into the ancient rue du Huchette in the Latin Quarter. The narrow alleys, romantically lit by gaslamps as always, were pulsing with touristic life, and off in the western distance, the sky still glowed a pinkish-orange from a big red sun that had earlier fallen into the atlantic horizon.

I sauntered happily along, without plan, without itinerary, without agenda, until the sound of Edith Piaf's unmistakable raspy voice led me to stop directly in front of an open archway, the entrance to a rather dark wine bar that had obviously been set up in what was once a wine cave, directly behind the Roman ruins in the beating heart of Paris.

I stepped inside without too much hesitation, and my glance went immediately to the winebar straight ahead, where I noticed a man standing by himself and, judging by the glass in hand, he was drinking a cognac. Other than the bartender, he was the only person there, very tall, very handsome, and dreadlocks extending at least six inches around his head like a black halo.

I went to claim a little round table in a corner, and then walked boldly up to the bar. I could feel the tall man watching me, probably looking at my very long silver hair, such a contrast to his own.

We made eye contact, and as soon as the bartender handed me a bordeaux, Monsieur Dreadlocks raised his glass in a traditional santé; I responded in kind and returned to my little round table in the corner.

Moments later, he unhesitatingly invited himself, with his own glass of wine, to sit across from me. Nothing dishonorable or unusual about that. Nor unexpected. The place had no bad vibes; and by now, the crackly sound system was offering appropriately soothing and jazzy flute music, filling this little cave bar with a soft and sensuous ambience.

Monsieur Dreadlocks seated across from me, I couldn't help noticing his attractive black features, and a smile that would have melted the hardest heart in a minute. We exchanged formalities and began the dialogue for the evening – in English! What is your name, Where are you from, What are YOU doing in Paris, and so on.

His name was Shamou, he was from Senegal, and he was, he said, a Wanderer!

"Is that all you do?" I asked.

"Oh no, Madame," he replied, with an almost Dickensian Uriah Heap humbleness in his voice. "I also think, and I dream; I dance now and then to make some money; I visit my thirteen-year-old daughter here in Paris; I laugh a lot, and I try to make others laugh. Laughter will help you live a long time, Madame."

Loving every word he said, and listening with curious interest, I told him, "You really have a fascinating . . . um . . . profession!?"

Throwing his head back, he burst into full laughter, and stroking the little barbîche on his chin with his philosophical thumb and forefinger said: "You call that a profession, Madame?"

He puzzled over that a moment, then, slanting his eyes down his face back toward me, offered: "I can see you worry too much. That is not a profession; that is just plain living."

His genuine profession, he nonetheless assured me, was dance; he was here in Paris with a small African traveling theatre troupe. He told me that during the past few years he had performed in Scotland, in Italy, and in Hungary! Interesting combination of countries, I thought.

Our wine glasses empty, I ordered a second round, which Shamou offered to pay for. I watched him reach down by his feet from where he pulled up a brilliantly embroidered cloth bag which, to me, looked altogether more like a piece of camel harness than a shoulder bag! With some fascination, I watched him open it, pull out a large well-aged leather-bound book (printed in French), between whose yellowed pages — he showed me — he had all his money hidden! The whole darn book was full of loose money! French paper money! I would guess he had at least several thousand francs in there.

Sensing my skepticism, he assured me, with his winsome smile, that I needn't worry about that either! It was his "bank", he said, and he needed always to carry it with him.

What is his real story, I'm wondering?! Does he even have an address on this planet? I was getting unbearably curious, but something about his illusive demeanor gave me a clue that I would not learn too much beyond what he had already told me. Though he appeared to be a very connected and engaging man, there was also something very distant about him, mysterious, almost perplexing — all of which was very hard on my old curiosity, and which he might well have interpreted as worry anyway.

"Where do you live now?" I dared to ask.

He leaned across the table with his beautiful smile and, gesturing into thin air with a long hand attached to the end of a very long arm, he began simply pointing right and left, saying in the gentlest voice imaginable: "Oh, sometimes I live here; sometimes I live there; sometimes I sit in a bar, like this, and I watch people all evening, and then I leave to sleep in a church pew at night, or on a park bench during the day. I am very lucky to have such a good life, Madame."

He looked at me with plenty of conviction but also somewhat inquisitively, as if he thought I expected a confirmation for what he had just told me.

For a moment, I found myself staring at him with considerable disbelief, trying to hide some laughter, yes, but I was also very much staring at him with admiration and honor, with fascination, perhaps even with a touch of envy at his beauty, his wit, his softness, his grace – AND his lifestyle! A different culture, a different attitude, a different approach, to be sure. I wanted to say he seemed almost enlightened, in a way that defied simple definition.

How extraordinary this was! We had both arrived at this tiny round table somewhere here in the ancient Roman heart of Paris, from two very distant and different parts of the world; we were two very different products of human creativity, yet so much about us was the same. Two civilizations quite removed from one another, yet strangely and beautifully bearing the same sensitivities. Fortunately, and magically, we had met here in Paris, devoid of a time and place where the proverbial race, age, color, creed, gender, and class distinction had very little to do with anything transpiring here in this moment.

There did, however, continue to be something about him I could not demystify, and it gave me cause to wonder – not worry, just wonder. I simply made a mental note of it.

The evening went on, the empty wine glasses growing in number, and I decided life could not be too much better, certainly not more enticing. At some point, after having stared all evening at that head of magnificent twisted filaments, I finally said to him with complete abandon: "Shamou, those dreadlocks, your hair – it all looks completely . . . chaotic! So different from your calm personality!"

"My hair chaotic, Madame?" he questioned, a little astonished at my description. "Oh no, not chaotic at all, perhaps . . . anarchistic!"

This time we both burst into raucous laughter and actually found we had stumbled upon a topic for possible debate for a few minutes: "What would life be like in a total Anarchy?" I asked him.

It became an altogether rather directionless and humorous spewing forth of tongue-slurred words concerning a subject neither of us, ultimately, knew that much about, nor had we ever experienced it. But it provided a perfect Parisian café moment.

The evening was moving onward, and it was about time for a somewhat concerned bartender to approach and bluntly inquire: "Who is paying for all these empty wine glasses, s'il vous plait?" Shamou very graciously agreed I was his guest, and he would do the honorable thing.

While the bartender went back to get the bill, I excused myself for a moment and stepped aside to go to the genderless pissoire. Shamou was left behind to take charge of things.

It was not more than a few minutes later when I returned to the little round table, with the bartender right on my heels. And I stopped dead in my tracks: Shamou . . . was GONE, nowhere in sight!

In shock, though not too surprised, I took a deep breath while the bartender stood there impatiently tapping his skeptical finger on the tabletop. Digging around in my bag, I found enough centimes and paper francs to pay the bill, and handed them to him.

Meanwhile, I sat down to contemplate my happy bewilderment; I finally figured out the mercurial mystery of Shamou, the professional Wanderer. I smiled, and thought: 'C'est la vie en Paris! The great capital of hope and the paradise of occasional mystery – or lawless madness!'

The bartender looked over to me, having pretty much sized up the situation, and decided to bring me a snifter with a snort of cognac – on the house! "Pour vous, Madame!" he gestured. I thanked him, and sniffed and sipped for one sweet-smelling cognac moment as I glanced around the room across the rim of my glass.

Over in another dark corner, a very handsome woman sat puffing on a cigarillo, with a distant but distinctly mysterious look on her face. I decided to disregard temptation and leave her to someone else's charms. I was quite satisfied for this evening.

What was that thing I once read about people being the happiest who don't HAVE the best of everything, but they MAKE the best of everything they have – an aphorism that somehow applied to this evening. Whatever else it might have been, it was definitely an interlude that completely arrested my adventurous spirit, and such opportunities are not offered to be denied.

Shamou, I hoped, was either off to visit his daughter, or, more likely, asleep on a church bench somewhere! I seriously contemplated stepping into St-Julian, the old stone church around the corner, to see if he just might be there . . . sleeping in a pew! On the other hand, I thought, he was probably 'reading' his money book in some other bar, charming another beautiful woman before disappearing inside the mystery of this great profession he called Wandering!

I raised my cognac glass to Shamou in absentia, thanked the bartender, who gave me one of those smiles, like "Yup, it's what happens," and I disappeared into the Paris night myself, feeling utter joy as I greeted a very bright gibbous moon hanging from an inky black sky high above the Centre Ville.

VII.
PARIS HAS BEEN
THERE FOREVER

INVENTORY THROUGH A HALF-MOON WINDOW

PARIS, FRANCE
April 2007
[inspired by Jacques Prévert]

AT MIDNIGHT
one old gas lamp, lit
      reflecting into my crooked wood-beamed room
      through ancient bubbled glasspanes
assorted architectural shapes
      triangles
      rectangles
      abstracts
      ovals
            formed inside four hundred years of whitewash
one narrow alley, cobbled
      glistening in the nightly mist
one tin roof, rippled
      two cats slinking to its edge
          one black
          one striped
             peering curiously at sounds below
one louvred window across the alley, open
      two lovers behind it, engaged
five night revelers in the alley, strolling
      one smoking
      one laughing
      two arm in arm

one following
one lone woman, sauntering
one amorous youth, hoping
one pair of stilettos, red
 left on the stoop
  worn down and liftless
one neon sign, orange
 wrapped around one word, franprix
one banner, red and black
 saying lizard lounge
three more revelers, inside
 with one tankard of ale in each left hand
one pigeon, audible
 above my window

nightfall

AT EARLY MORNING
a ray of light, dawn
two pigeons, visible
one noisy trash truck, green
two drivers, arguing
four garbage cans, filled
 lids way up
one supermarche door, open
one door guard, half interested
three pigeons, very visible

AT DAYTIME
one big superette window, shiny clean
 behind it

seventeen mangos, yellow-green
    in circular arrangement
twelve apples, red
    in perfect alignment
three baguettes, crisp
    in a basket
one mister, walking by
one beret, on mister's head
one madam, in a hurried step
one pair of dolce jeans, on madam's hip
one more pigeon, flying
one artist, sketching
    a 17th century door
one lovely lady, meandering
    yellow daffodil in hand
one baggy lady, attached to a leash
    pulled by a pekingese
one baby, squealing
one mother, behind it
    licking berthillon icecream
several more pigeons, scurrying

AT DUSK
one day of good things
one moment of reflective silence
one four-hundred-year-old cityscape
one more day in Paris
one grateful heart

ON BAUDELAIRE'S BENCH

PARIS, FRANCE
May 2010

Invariably, the last day arrives, with every visit to Paris. For me, it becomes the last day to wander, to relax, and to soak in, for a few more hours, the Paris I grow to love more each time I go. Over dozens of visits, I have walked many romantic and rustic kilometers within her periphery, and so this visit has added a few more special memories.

I had given myself a gift as far as apartments go — a Seventeenth Century gem in the crown of central Paris, in the very center of Île St Louis itself. The flat was elegantly furnished with original art deco pieces by its dedicated owners, who are art lovers and art collectors. The lady of the house is also a world renowned artist photographer, and she had decorated the flat with exclusive originals from her collection. Living in this flat I truly felt as if I was a Parisian living in Paris, one of the two times amidst the many. This location provided a wondrous thing: the time-honored privacy I desired at day, and it allowed me to walk to places very nearby at night, a much-loved and enchanting exercise for me, near the midnight hour, when night has fallen, and the streets of Paris become one's own. The street lamps have all snapped on, and beams of light everywhere illuminate monuments and building façades, making them look like pieces of a stage set for living theatre. It is almost impossible to comprehend her unique beauty at such times, but I can feel it, strolling in her midst with total freedom and absence of purpose. As a poet, which I claim in small part to be, an evening such as this in Paris is very poetic.

I agree with people who have written countless times in numerous books that daylight flattens and hardens Paris, whereas nightlight brings out the bends and recesses, the secret interiors, not to mention the sensuously slithering quality of Madame Seine, herself. She flows in silence, in unnoticeable movement. Late evening is also a time within the twenty-fourhour cycle that is stripped of superfluous noise. The guided bus groups that fill the streets have faded away. It is a time when the city's magic steals back. It is a time when one can have a true twilight epiphany in the nighttime ambience.

~ ~ ~ ~ ~ ~ ~

Passing the splendorously majestic Hôtel de Ville, strolling alongside the venerable Seine, and crossing the other old bridge, Pont Marie, onto the Île Saint-Louis, I turned left, casting off toward the eastern half of the island where a mottled stone bench awaited my arrival under a streetlamp that threw a distinct yellowish light across the cobbled sidewalk.

I smiled, remembering reading about this old bridge, built in 1614 and, until several hundred years ago, the only crossing from Île Saint-Louis to the "mainland" — as Paris was referred to. During the early 1800s, when this island was still a colony with its very own government separate from the City of Paris, the ladies on the Île Saint-Louis would dress up for the day, meet at the carrefour (the main four corners in the very middle of the island), and they would say: "Today we are going to Paris!"

A sweet anecdote, to be sure, and I was reminded just here and now of what my dear friend Bruno, a French painter living in southwest France, had told me many years ago, while we sat in a tiny café on the Île, reminiscing about our many adventures together in Paris. In his uniquely humorous way, he described to me: "Yes, in France everything is divided into regions, departments, districts, municipalities, towns, communes, villages, cafés, and telephone kiosks. And each of these has its own government."

~ ~ ~ ~ ~ ~ ~

I have always loved this location by the Pont Marie, near a wide and romantic stairwell that descends to the Seine's edge. From this bench, I can observe the purest reflection of Pont Marie at a time in the night when the Seine becomes like a glass mirror. There is no wind, there are no ripples on the moving water. The behemoth babbling bateaux mouches have anchored down for the night somewhere upstream, and I can sit here, on this old stone bench and enjoy a perfect moment without commotion and blinding reflective boat lights.

'My' stone bench of choice happens also to be on the quai d'Anjou, adjacent to a notorious address, No. 17, the mansion once inhabited, several floors up, by the inveterate noctambulist, the Nineteenth Century French poet and notable essayist, Charles Baudelaire, a true Parisian and poet of the city. The place became his true den of iniquity as he squandered his hated stepfather's inheritance and indulged in the then-common absinthe and opium orgies with his contemporary cronies, Gautier, Rimbaud, Verlaine, Mallarmé, Balzac, Flaubert, and the many others.

It was here he had written his now well-known and much-loved epic, "Les Fleurs du Mal" ("The Flowers of Evil"), expressing the little-loved changing nature of beauty in modern, industrialized, Paris during the Nineteenth Century. I had some time ago read the George Dillon translation of Baudelaire's fascinating, though dark, series of these prose poems, written in this very dwelling, with a profoundly beautiful introduction, in the final 1936 publication, by Edna St. Vincent Millay, a poet I greatly admire. I was not only slightly pleased to have found a first-print edition of this publication, safely locked behind a glass-windowed bookcase in a dusty second-hand book nook, in Montparnasse, more than fifteen years ago. It now inhabits a space in my own glass-windowed case, across the sea, in San Francisco.

On this evening I was mesmerized by the beautiful Seine as she flowed steadily and quietly past me under and beyond Pont Marie and onward toward some outlet to the northern seas. I was quietly thinking how much life she has seen, and how she symbolizes the seconds and minutes, the months and years, indeed the centuries that disappear – all too quickly.

In the midst of my reverie, contemplating the mercurial quickness of time and life, of duration and being, and thinking about the last five hundred years of history even just right here on the island, two young rollerbladers bumped by on the stone cobbles. The rattling sound broke my spell and put a big smile on my face. In that moment, suddenly, the ancient past and the modern present had magically crossed the barrier of time in a split second. And just then, as I looked behind me and upward, I could see gangly old Baudelaire himself, hanging off his window ledge, waving. "C'est la vie!" he chuckled cynically, "Ici une seconde et allé le prochain." ("That's life; here one second and gone the next!")

All the more reason to enjoy every minute of it while I'm here, I thought.

On my way to home, I took a long round-about detour and headed to Her Serene Ladyship, la Notre Dame. I had not been on the plaza in front of the main entrance at the midnight hour for a long time. This evening, the crowded masses had long departed, and as if ordained by the magical muses, only two people besides me were there. The lights of the cathedral had gone dark, and the gas lights around the plaza were giving the Old Lady a much-needed and restful repose. A perfect ambience of peace and calm, and difficult to believe hundreds, even thousands, would once again be descending upon this hallowed spot on the planet in just a few more hours. In close to thirty years of visiting and living in Paris, I had never seen this emptiness before; but I had also never made an effort to be here at this time of night. This night, I stood freely and unhurried on the brass carved Kilometre Zero on the square facing the main entrance of Notre Dame cathedral, the official centre of the city of Paris. The only heart beating right there at that moment was my own. The regal Notre Dame looked so relieved inside the night's emptiness, retreated, into a virtual state of gathering back her energy and rejuvenating for the next day's onslaught.

Eventually, I sauntered back to Bourg Tibourg, to the terrasse of Café

Féria in my neighborhood, to indulge in my last nightly verre du bordeaux for this time. The lovely young waitress, Marie-Eva, who had begun to recognize me from the frequent late-night visits, waved from the doorway to say she'd bring it right out.

~ ~ ~ ~ ~ ~ ~

And so this hourney was, as they always were, another journey like none other I had experienced, another I would remember with a particular fondness. Whether it's possible for me to love Paris more each time I go? Without question. But just now, I needed to go home to my flat, pack all my memories, my feelings, my intimate secrets, my new ideas, my new loves, my dreams of the heart, my celebrations and inspirations, and head back to the airport, for those grueling security checks followed by eleven tortured hours of flying in peasant class!!

As I commenced with the packing, I was recalling the stay. One thing I did not need to pack in my suitcase, but that I kept permanently embossed upon my mind was the quote from Victor Hugo framed and hanging on the wall just inside the door of his Place des Vosges residence: "There is nothing so fantastic, nothing so tragic, nothing so superb, as Paris!"

Of course, I agreed.

~ ~ ~ ~ ~ ~ ~

Meanwhile, Madame la Seine weeps at the mention of my departure, the cobbles retract, the wine bar down on the terrace goes bankrupt in my absence, and my favorite bench on the quai d'Anjou stands alone and empty for another year. As to Baudelaire, he just keeps reminding me, in his own inimitable words, that the sun at close of day reflects "nothing else but grace and measure, richness, quietness, and pleasure." And at dawn, old Paris rises once more, picks up its tools, and he will add:

". . . and, over the deserted Seine,
Yawning, rubbing its eyes,
     slouches forth to work again."

VIII.
IN REMEMBRANCE
OF MOM AND DAD

DORIS

THE NEW FOREST, ENGLAND
August 1990

[This episode is extracted from a much longer and more comprehensive story, so I have attempted to put the earlier parts in very brief chronological order, and mostly describe here the one and only enchanted meeting, after several decades, between my mother and Doris Westerhoff. Sadly, but joyfully, it was toward the end of both their lives.]

This story had its beginnings somewhere between the two world wars. The aftermath of World War I had wreaked havoc upon the colonies of southern Ukraine. Factions of the Bolshevik Revolution were moving southward in Russia, harassing and killing innocent people and conscientious objectors along the Black Sea. Massive migrations were on-going, one such refugee movement including my mother and her parents, from South Russia to Latvia by train, and by ship through the Baltic Sea, across the North Sea, and eventually to Canada, via England.

My earliest recollection of this story has me at seven years of age, about 1947, when Dad came home one day from the General Store, a mile down the country road, with a few food supplies and an airmail letter-sized envelope. The letter was addressed to Tina Engbrecht, Winkler, Canada. On the other side of the envelope, the return address must have offered some magical word, and I saw tears in my mother's eyes — which made me wonder immediately. I had never seen my mother cry!

Given that Mom was no longer an Engbrecht, it was miracle enough that this letter had found her with such a sparse address, but the bigger miracle was that it had come from South England across the sea, from Doris, the waitress and first-aid attendant who had befriended my mother during a six-month encampment of several thousand Russian refugees in Southampton, more than two decades ago, in 1926.

~ ~ ~ ~ ~ ~ ~

Time went on, I was a teenager in a little one-room country school house. Whenever the opportunity presented itself during long Winter months, I began asking Mom about this friend, the arrival of whose letter had elicited tears I remembered seeing long ago. Mom, smiling proudly at me, her daughter, and wanting to satisfy my curiosity, told me this amazing story, little by little.

We begin with Mom's childhood memory of an endless journey across turbulent seas, hundreds of children and their parents being crowded into the bottom of a big ship, most of them sleeping on unswept wood floors and elders in the few available bunkers. Undernourished people, struck down from motion sickness, were running high fevers. Many of them were extremely underfed and frightened which, naturally, left them vulnerable to every possible disease that could incubate happily inside their tired and malnourished bodies. Scurvy and tuberculosis became rampant and epidemic, forcing the ship to dock in Southampton Harbor for six months. All passengers were off-loaded and quarantined in a defunct World War I air hangar. Each family was given a space, sparsely but adequately furnished, and separated from the next by room dividers crudely constructed of cardboard. The British Government's port authorities provided manual services, including food, health aids, and clothing. Each family was assigned one assistant for such services.

A woman named Doris Westerhoff, assigned to the my grandparents' space, came into my mother's life. Doris was twenty-three years of age, and Mom was ten. A very special connection developed between the two — a separate and touching story exists about this elsewhere in my journals — with Doris ultimately asking my grandparents if she might adopt my mother, not an uncommon request during those troubled and tumultuous times. In the end, however, Mom arrived in Manitoba, Canada, with her family, and contact between the two was severed for all intents and purposes. Age discrepancy alone would have defied that possibility.

A little known fact, however, would change that impossibility around. About ten years after the family's arrival in Canada, my mother was given a small piece of paper that had been found by her oldest brother amongst old immigration documents. On it was written Doris's address, in her own handwriting, and a short note asking Mom's brother (already seventeen years in age at the time) to give it to his youngest sister, my mother, when she was able to read and write, with the hope that they would perhaps one day find one another again. This miraculous little piece of paper in hand, Mom, now aged twenty, immediately set about trying to mail letters overseas to Doris. To put it into better perspective, it was 1936, my mother was dating my father, and they married in 1938. World War II began in 1939.

Many attempts were made by my mother to reconnect with Doris, but through the trials and tribulations of looming war, there were many misses, many returns of letters marked undeliverable. Over time, Mom had also created several goodwill packages for Doris, and sent them off to 347 Southampton Road via sea mail, never really knowing if anything arrived.

Until this letter came one day, in 1947. The connection with Doris was thus miraculously re-ignited, approximately twenty-one years later.

Letters began traveling back and forth regularly between Mom and Doris, at 374 Southampton Road in Eastleigh. It remained strictly a correspondence friendship; no thought was ever given to the idea of the two of them seeing one another again. It was not even mentioned in their letters. I have many of them.

Then, one day, fate turned things around and an opportunity presented itself in the Summer of 1990. My mother, Katherine Epp, was now seventy-four years of age, and Doris was eighty-seven. They had not seen one another for sixty-four years.

Momentarily backtracking nearly twenty years to 1971, I was living in Munich, Germany, and decided one late Spring it was time to bridge the span of so many years between the Epps in Canada and the Westerhoffs in England. I appointed myself the personal emissary for this mission and set off, determined to meet, face to face, this mystery family, known but unknown. Arrangements were made, and a ferryboat crossing on the English Channel landed me at Dover. There I embarked on a train to London's Victoria Station, where I was to be met by Donald, the older son. *[An interesting side note here is that Donald and I had also been corresponding back and forth, though we, too, had never met.]* Walking along an endless train station platform, I looked for someone resembling the photo of Donald I had with me. I came upon a paging booth and was about to have his name called, when I thought I recognized him from the back, a surprisingly tall man. I tapped him on the shoulder, and he turned around and said: "Are you Erika?"

"Indeed I am; and I guess you're Donald!" In good old-fashioned Victorian English style, we did not hug! My tongue was tied, but some typical chit-chat ensued, and then we were back on another train that took us all the way South toward Eastleigh. Sitting next to one another on the train, I kept thinking how strange, yet how familiar, this was. Over easily four decades, we had come to know one another, in fact, grown up together, through an amazing letter correspondence, but neither of us had ever seen one another, nor met in person.

Soon enough we arrived in Eastleigh, the home of Doris. I cannot adequately describe my unprecedented feeling, walking up the sidewalk to the house at the address 374 Southampton Road, which I had written countless times on those old-fashioned thin blue envelopes with red-striped borders. The fact that I was about to deliver greetings in person, on behalf of my mother, at that exact same address, was a gripping moment. Donald stayed back, near the car. I knocked the clacker on the door, and a few seconds later, my heart pounding inside me, Doris opened, still wiping her hands on her apron, having just washed up the supper dishes. Her head tilted upward as she stared at me through her bi-focal glasses, she smiled broadly: "So you are Erika, Katherine's daughter," she said, reaching over for a slight handshake. "Oh, I can't believe it. Please come in!" As I think back on that moment now, it must have been an odd sensation for Doris, now aged sixty-eight, who had known my mother as a young girl of ten, and now was seeing that young girl's grown daughter at more than twice the age.

For five wonderful days I visited with Doris and her husband Bert, a retired navy mechanic, and with Donald, his young wife, Anne, and their firstborn, a daughter named Shirley. There was also Donald's younger brother Gerald. It was a time of tremendous elation and animated conversation as we all tried to catch up on at least four decades and three generations of respective family history. Doris had brought down from her attic a box of old photographs, plus a raft of letters, most of them from my mother to Doris, and a few from us kids as well. They were her treasures, she said. Sadly, I was not the eventual recipient of those, but my mind recorded enough facts and visuals to recreate the story. It hadn't occurred to me then that perhaps copies could have been made of a few of them.

So the visit was spent as much getting acquainted as reminiscing, and each exclamation ended with the wish that it might somehow, someday, be possible for Doris and my mother to reunite.

~ ~ ~ ~ ~ ~ ~

Moving forward to 1988, eighteen years after this initial visit, I was living in San Francisco, and decided to go back to South England once more on my own, to visit with the Westerhoff clan. Doris's husband Bert had passed on, and it was great to meet a new generation now, Shirley and Alan, the two grown children of Donald and Anne, and Gerald's wife Diana and their daughter Hannah. During this particular visit, Donald and I finally decreed it was essential; time was marching on and the two matriarchs of the Epp/ Westerhoff households must meet in person. Both were getting on in age and Doris was becoming very frail, and somewhat forgetful. The decision was made that I would bring my mother to England for this purpose, as she was still in very good physical health, and mentally very alert.

"Can it really be done?" Donald wondered, looking directly at me.

"Yes, of course," I said. "Frankly, I suddenly have no idea why there has been so much hesitation around this, especially in recent years." I understood that once, long ago, such a journey seemed close to impossible for the two ladies, each within their particular life circumstances. But I firmly believed I could convince my mother to do this as long as I accompanied her.

~ ~ ~ ~ ~ ~ ~

Two years later, in the Summer of 1990, I at last flew up to Central Canada to prepare my mother and pack her up for this extraordinary journey to South England! We spent two days planning things, and I recall she showed little discomposure even if she was somewhat daunted by the idea of taking this long journey back across the sea, bearing in mind the only impression she had of that long ago event was as a child in the bottom of a ship that not only suffered through illness and family losses during six months in Southampton, but also took weeks to arrive at its destination. Since that time, she had never sailed across the Atlantic again; in fact she had flown only very few times, and very short distances.

Mom was now seventy-four. On the eve of our departure, I sat down with her over a glass of wine and asked her to tell me her feelings, tell me what was on her mind about this historical journey she was about to embark upon. Her response was beautiful and reflective: "When I was young and small, growing up on the same farm where you were born, everything in the world seemed big and impossible to overcome or achieve. An ocean wasn't crossable, another country was somewhere else and too far distant on the planet, not within reach. A country was something I saw in geography books and on world maps on school walls. Travel was imaginary for me in the wilderness of Central Canada, unless we were going by horse and buggy to the grandparent's farm a few miles down a bumpy country road."

For my part, I also wanted to share with Mom what I was thinking, on the eve of her big adventure: "It wasn't until I was a teenager that you had begun explaining why Doris Westerhoff was in your life, and why she had taken up such prominence in it. As you remember, I listened to you, always, with rapt attention. I loved hearing your stories about the migration from Russia to Canada, and particularly the story you recounted about living in the hangar with several thousand refugees, where you met Doris, the big reason for our return journey now."

That evening, I wrote in my journal:

> How almost impossible to realize this evening that I am taking my dear mother across the sea to reunite with noble Doris, sixty-four years later, and finally tying together the dangling threads of an unusual piece of both our families' histories.

~ ~ ~ ~ ~ ~ ~

By a fluke of luck, and upon taking a look at my elderly mother, the British Airways employee at Toronto Airport decided he would place us in first class — a rare favor in the pre-upgrade-war days. My mother had no idea what a gift she had received, this being her first trans-oceanic flight ever. Though awed by it all, she took it to be quite normal, more than adequate leg room, seat backs that shifted into all kinds of comfortable positions, meals served on linen clothes with real china and silverware, and a choice of three entrees on the menu. A proper royal indulgence for her, topped off with a great Irish Creme, which Mom promptly got hooked on, not having any idea it was a spirited drink. It did allow her a nice sleep for most of the flying hours. She awoke at one point in mid-flight and said: "I always wondered what it felt like to be on a cloud!"

Our descent into London was greeted by a rare clear, bright, sunny morning, giving Mom the perfect chance of her lifetime to see Queen Elizabeth's entire Buckingham Palace from the air.

We got waved through customs with a smile, and charmed through the exit gate. All of London was set and staged for my beautiful mother to see, firsthand. It would be a visit she would later call a dream. A stroll through Westminster Abbey's Poets' Corner, past the Fountain at Buckingham Palace, and a serious study of St. Paul's Dome, all remained spellbound favorites for her.

~ ~ ~ ~ ~ ~ ~

A good night's sleep was essential for her, for both of us, as the next day meant getting on the train to South England, to the New Forest, the area where all the Westerhoffs now lived, near a town called Ringwood. I watched Mom on that train; I could tell she was beginning to feel anxious as the meeting with Doris loomed ever nearer. We sat in a very shiny booth, with a table upon which to rest our elbows, while we watched a rather dull and industrial countryside reel by. Short of an hour, we reached the village of Brockhampton, where Donald had agreed to meet us, on Track Two, right by the public telephone booth!

The instant the train began slowing down, Mom's face lit up like the sun. "Are we here?" she asked. "I can feel my heart beating, fast." She could hardly contain herself. After six decades, all the way back to south England to meet an unusual friend, who could have?!

Through the window of the train, I had noticed Donald on the platform, all dressed in shirt and tie, waiting. When the door of the train opened, I ushered Mom to step down with her small bag in hand. Donald, whom she did not know, and I had choreographed this entire visit for her from this stage onward. We wanted her to be surprised all the way. At this point, Donald came up to her saying: "Pardon me, madam, may I assist you?"

Mother, somewhat startled, looked at me in all innocence saying: "There are such nice people in England." She had no idea, and it wasn't until a few steps further, with Donald still walking beside her, that it occurred to her: "Oh my goodness; are you Donald?" And the alligator tears welled up. Surprised and speechless, she stood for a moment, to look around, completely transfixed. She had arrived at her destination, and Donald was absolute living proof of the miracle she was about to experience within the next twenty-four hours.

"Where is 374 Southampton Road?" she wanted to know, in her very first minute here.

"You'll see it, Mom! I promise," I assured her.

Settled in Donald's car at last, we were off, into a world of blind wonder, Mom completely bewildered and baffled. Sitting on 'the wrong side of the car', as she remarked, didn't do much to help her get her bearings. These next days, I would have a great time watching her from the back seat as she gazed out the window, mystified, and disconcerted, questioning everything. I could see a new human being evolving from her; that unrestrained and unrepressed childlike wonder from long ago in her carefree world in Russia had resurfaced for her, here on this journey. I was pleased for her, so pleased. Not to mention, impressed with her high energy. I could see how something way outside her domestic confinement back home had taken her over, totally manipulated her feelings. And how she loved the drive through the New Forest to get to Donald's house, with the many ponies running wild, and the whole enchantment of an ancient world.

~ ~ ~ ~ ~ ~ ~

Next day, we were finally on our way to experience the big moment: the two ladies coming face to face! On the way over, Donald thought it would be interesting for Mom to see the old hangar where this entire story began, now sixty-four years ago. The hangar was indeed there, dismal and dilapidated, but for some reason, Mom didn't want to get out of the car. She looked at it through the car window, in some disbelief, probably quietly trying to find a realistic memory of it. She told me later she wasn't sure what to make of the place, realizing she was a little girl when she was last there, never really knowing in her child's mind where she was, or had been, or even why.

Fortunately, we needed to pass by the old 374 Southampton Road address as well, and as Donald slowed down some, Mom felt a lump in her throat and a twinge in her heart. The way she always did when things defied description for her, she held her fingers to her chin and stared with big eyes in innocent wonder and disbelief at the address. To be within a few feet of the place to where all those letters and packages had been delivered, where she had spent time as a young girl on weekends with Doris. It all seemed a little overwhelming just now as a tear trickled slowly down her cheek.

Mom sat very still. I knew more than anything she was thinking and wondering about Doris. Now she couldn't wait to see her, and actually I told Donald we had tortured her long enough with the wait.

We arrived at the complex where Doris was now staying, a home for aging and afflicted people. Donald took my mother by the arm and guided her up the steps and inside the lobby. I stayed just a few steps behind. We didn't want to confuse Doris, who had already met me several times, the last time being just two years prior, as she might think this was me again. While walking into the building, Donald told me in order to set this up he had called the lady warden earlier, wanting her to make sure Doris was wearing a pretty dress because he was bringing a friend to tea.

By now, I was jittery as well. From a distance of about ten feet behind Mom, a ton of emotion was bubbling inside me.

At last we were at Doris's door, which Donald unlocked, and then opened it wide. My breath stopped as I watched the richest moment transpire: Mom seemed frozen to her spot in the doorway, with her hand across her mouth, and utterly speechless, and then she entered the room all the way and stepped toward Doris, who seemed hypnotized, or paralyzed as if from a bolt of lightning. Mom, not exactly sure what to do, studied the situation as best she could; she had been warned that Doris was experiencing some difficulty with memory.

And then Doris, after staring at Mom for what seemed an eternity, suddenly grabbed Mom's hands and said: "Katherine, it's you!"

She had recognized her!

This was, of course, followed by all the nervous laughter, the tears, and, surprisingly, a long reciprocal hug. Both stared at one another, in complete disbelief. It was almost painful, and again I wondered why we hadn't just made this happen sooner. This moment seemed almost unfair. Right now, neither knew what to say to the other, and after a few minutes of 'ohs' and longer 'ooooh's, Donald and I escorted our respective Moms to two armchairs standing side by side. It was then I realized each one was by pure coincidence wearing a turquoise dress, and once they saw that themselves, they giggled together like two young girls. It took a very long time for them to let go of each other's handclasp, as, little by little, moments of mental orientation from long ago came into play. Slowly, bits and pieces of conversation and dialogue began.

I was standing across the room with a notebook, and Donald had his camera. I recorded their dialogue in shorthand, recording Doris in her own native English dialect.

Mother: *[looking at Doris in disbelief, smiling]* "I just can't believe it!"

Doris: *[laughing]* "Katherine, y'was just a little girl then . . . "

Mother: "Yes, and we ate at a long table, do you remember?" *[more laughter, every little utterance followed by laughter!]*

Doris: "Yehhhs."

Mother: "And after every meal, I stacked the dishes at the end of the table, and you took them to the kitchen."

Doris: "Yehhhs. You stacked the dinner plates then?! Y'was just a little girl then!? I remember. Y'was just ten or so. Yehhhs!"

Mother: "Yes, that's right."

Doris: "Y'followed me everywhere, y'was just a little girl. Brought me bike over to me, y'did, yehhhs, and y'followed me 'round when y'was just little, then."

Mother: "Yes, I remember. Did you know I sneaked into the kitchen and stole a bread roll and toasted it by the ashes *[Mom meant embers]*, and you caught me doing it?"

Doris: *[her eyes filled with surprise]* "Oh dear, yehhhs. Oh you was so pretty, and scared . . . "

[A small pause.]

Mother: *[seriously now, looking into Doris's eyes]* "You were always my friend, ever since I was a little girl. All the letters you sent to Canada, and then your children began writing to my children, all these years."

Doris: "I remember y'sent packages in the war, yehhhs, in the war. Donald, d'you remember then?!"

Donald: *[nodding affirmative]*

Doris: *[looking past Donald, at me now]* "Who's this then?"

[Reminder: though she had already met me several times in years past, today confused her, as we suspected, because both I and my mother were here at the same time. Actually years ago, Doris had already thought I was Katherine.]

Mother: "That's Erika."

Doris: "Oh yehhhs. Y'was visitin' here last time . . . Was y'here with Donald then . . . ?"

Doris: *[looking back at Mom again]* "You're Katherine. Yehhhs. I remember when y'was a young girl. How old was you then? You was just little, and you's with a brother, or so?!"

Mother: "Yes, I was ten, and I was with my oldest brother."

Doris: "I remember. I took you to me house in Eastleigh. You couldn't speak English, y'know. Yehhhs. You was just a little girl. Couldn't speak English. Yehhhs. You was all from a big boat in Southampton."

At this point, the conversation had begun to slow down momentarily, so my mother began presenting Doris with a few gifts she had brought, handmade by herself. A knitted afghan, for the top of the bed, and a pillow case she also knitted, with the pillow already in it, and finally, a pair of blue knitted foot slippers. Doris kept putting the gifts behind her on the bed, remaining totally ecstatic with all the excitement and activity, seldom letting her gaze fall away from my mother. Mom was fascinated, watching Doris, who seemed in and out of memory snatches, trying to recall a whole lifetime ago, and just being so tickled about this visit that she seemed slightly out of focus.

Eventually, the same old picture box and all the albums, ancient and recent, were hauled out once more from under the bed, and the rest of that visit was spent reminiscing over photos. Doris showed Mom a picture of Bert, saying: "That's my husband Bert, d'you remember? That was so long ago."

Every so often, Doris would look back at Mom and say: "You was just a little girl then. How old was you then? Can't believe it. Y'would come with me on me bike to Eastleigh, d'you remember then?"

And so the few hours of togetherness between them were spent. On the next visit, Doris had draped the afghan across her bed, and the pillow was in its place at the head of the bed. And next to the pillow, the sweetest thing, those little slippers, as if they belonged to Cinderella. She said she was never going to wear them. She tried to tell us she was going to hold them in her sleep rather than wear them.

~ ~ ~ ~ ~ ~ ~

There were three visits in all. By the third visit, alas, the final one forever, Doris's mind had become quite stimulated, and she was beginning to remember more long-ago things, though she would repeat them numerous times in the meeting.

The indelible imprint upon my own mind about this scene was the two of them sitting side by side, as close as they could physically sit, both in their turquoise dresses, looking like twins with their white short curly hair, blue eyes, and holding hands, smiling, laughing, giggling, and feeling utterly overjoyed, each moment painted with many variations and levels of disbelief. A picture worth a million words.

The last goodbye was difficult, but the dream had come true, and a wonderful mission, a journey, had been accomplished. Some kind of closure had been experienced, certainly for my mother. Still it was an onerous situation for her to comprehend. The hello had barely happened, and already the goodbye had transpired. It was all too much of a time-warp.

There was an endearing goodbye hug, and we began the walk down the hallway. Doris, thankfully, didn't understand that this would be Mom's last visit. Standing in the door of her apartment, her big black purse across her right arm (whose sole content was one house key), she smiled and waved until we were out of sight. She had been full of humor and warmth, and, I daresay, appreciation. It was that same smile and that same waving of the hand that I remembered from eighteen years before when I met her for the first time in Eastleigh. And I'm sure I can't be too far wrong in conjecturing that it was the same smile and the same hand waving that my mother remembered when she would watch Doris pedal across that bridge from the hangar, many decades ago, in Southampton.

~ ~ ~ ~ ~ ~ ~

I heard from Donald several weeks later that Doris had called numerous times, somewhat confused and wondering what time Katherine was returning for a visit, was Katherine going to stay in England for a while so they could visit some more, and so on. I felt sad for Doris, but I knew Mom understood, and she was very pleased. Mom told me on the flight home, "The visit was just long enough, and one I will never forget."

~ ~ ~ ~ ~ ~ ~

I wrote into my journal after the last visit:

If life is a web of mingled yarns, Mom has knitted a perfect cloth on this journey; she crossed her own desert and reached her own destiny. In the image and words of Longfellow, 'that which the fountain had sent forth returned again to the fountain'.

I was proud to have taken my mother on this journey, back to the source and the reason for so much joy in her long life. Her ability to have been able to transfer herself completely to that place and experience of long ago, away from her daily domestic life, remained the epithet for the rest of her life.

~ ~ ~ ~ ~ ~ ~

Within the next year, mother's dear friend, Doris Westerhoff, passed away. The memory of her remained a living one for my mother, until she, herself, passed away eleven years later.

Lichtenau Exit

THE BLACK SEA, UKRAINE
June 2004

[What follows is the last part of a very long story about the journey to the Black Sea with my father. This episode includes an abbreviated version of visits to the villages of Lindenau, where he was born, and Tiegerweide, where he grew up. It ends with the special circumstances and celebrations surrounding the visit to our third and last village, Lichtenau, from where Dad and his parents and siblings left Russia in 1924.]

~ ~ ~ ~ ~ ~ ~

It was a chilled and rainy April evening in Paris. I was entertaining some of my Parisian friends when the phone rang.

"Hello there, daughter! It's your Dad calling from Winnipeg!"

Dad never ever called me in Paris, but detecting unusual excitement in his voice, it wouldn't be bad news, I guessed.

"Hey Dad, what's up? How great to hear you!"

"Well, daughter, you know I just turned ninety, and before too much more time gets away from me, I was hoping you would come with me to South Russia, to the Ukraine, sometime this Summer. I want to go back to the Molotschna Colony, to Lindenau where I was born, to Tiegerweide where I was raised, and to Lichtenau, from where the train left for Latvia with all of us onboard. Do you think we can do it? It would be in celebration of my ninetieth birthday, and my gift to you for being my guide."

There was an almost breathless pause on the phone line while I tried as quickly as possible to assemble this in my brain before saying: "Dad! Yes! I will go with you. Thank you! Wow! Yes, we can do it! We can absolutely do it. But I would prefer to hear you say this is your gift to me for being my father! The guide part is easy."

He laughed that special laugh I will always remember about him. "Great," he said. "When do you get back from Paris? We don't have too much time to make arrangements."

And he was right, but I was booked to stay in Paris until end May, which I did, and that would still leave me with several weeks in San Francisco to turn around and prepare for this incredible journey — an experience made all the better because I would be alongside my father, a late-in-life enthusiastic traveler himself.

I called Dad a few days after I returned from Paris: "Hey, Dad, have you been diligent about gathering information for our trip?" I could hear a small hesitation in his voice, sensing there was something in the back of his mind about this trip he was not telling me, some secret, but perhaps that was conjecture, I wasn't sure.

"What information do I need, daughter? I was born there, and I remember certain buildings and creeks and a few paths to my cousin's house," he blew back. "I've been thinking a lot about my earliest childhood, being forced to leave such an idyllic place as the Black Sea and, in spirit, never being able therefore to completely disconnect from it."

"I understand," I said, "so here's what I've figured out. We will be able to fly as far as Kiev, via Toronto and Frankfurt, then we need to take a very long train ride to the last biggish town before the colonies — that would be Zaporozhye. After that, there are no numbered roads or signed highways along the Dnieper River to your colony, the Molotschna, so we can't do this alone. So I suggest I look into hiring two university students in Kiev, who speak English, and who know their way around this wilderness of the Black Sea colonies. What do you think?"

"Daughter, you set it up, and do whatever it takes to get us there. I really like the idea of hiring university students. Maybe I can practice some Russian with them." Dad was obviously only interested in getting there, and didn't worry about any obstacles or issues we might encounter along the way.

I spent a few days trying to make contact with some university offices in Kiev, and eventually, and miraculously, thanks to the wonderful tool of internet research, landed via email connection in a Department of International Cooperation at the Taras Shevchenko National University of Kiev, an old established university by all historical accounts. Through this International Cooperation Department, I was able to procure for a summertime hire two students, both of whom spoke sufficient English, and who apparently were acquainted well enough with the landscape of the southern colonies to guide us there, through, and back. With that little miracle in place, I purchased two train tickets on line to get Dad and myself from Kiev to Zaporozhye, and there the two students would meet us with a van, at the train station itself, and drive us anywhere we wished, first off to the Intourist Hotel in downtown Zaporozhye itself, where I had made reservations to stay for a week.

~ ~ ~ ~ ~ ~ ~

A total of thirty-six hours of waiting in and flying through several airports, landed us in Kiev, feeling very worn and tired. I'll never forget Dad's comment as we disembarked onto the tarmac in Kiev's airport: "Ah, we are here. Isn't this just wonderful!? Mother Russia!" he exclaimed, as he bent down and touched the ground.

It took a bit of doing, but given Dad's age, I had arranged, via the Lufthansa information desk in Kiev's airport, for a taxi to meet us and take us to our hotel in downtown Kiev. And by the good graces of many angels, there, several meters immediately in front of us, stood a young man wearing a white T-shirt and jeans, holding up a sign that said "John i Erika." He was Yevgeny and delivered us efficiently to our hotel, a grand old Kiev hotel, with all the amenities necessary to provide a comfortable evening and night for two worn travelers.

The following morning, Yevgeny was waiting for us at the front of the hotel to take us to the handsome and historic Kiev train station, the Pivdenny Vokzal. With all the enthusiasm Dad could muster, after that long journey from Central Canada to South Russia, he hoisted his somewhat tired frame up the train steps, ambled over to our assigned cabin, and with that, his dream of seeing the vast and splendid steppes of the Ukraine would begin. The train whistle blew, and we were off to Zaporozhye.

About five hours later, after crossing the Dnieper River on a vertiginously high concrete and steel bridge, we reached Zaporozhye, enshrouded under a gray sky. A few minutes of easing into the train station — a moment which always manages to conjure romance from old movies — and we had arrived. "Dad," I said, "we are here, at the edge of the colonies, which you've been waiting to see for the past eighty years!" We exited the train, each with our one bag in tow. And then the great prize. What a relief it was, after such a long journey, to be greeted by two smiling young gentlemen students, both in their mid-twenties, each carrying a placard, once again reading "Erika i John." From the smiles on our faces, they could tell it was us, and I'll never forget how they came forward, with their hearty and warm handshakes, and a genuinely enthusiastic reception.

"Welcome, welcome," the taller one said to Dad. "I am Aleksei, and he is my companion, Vadim," he said, pointing to the other student. "We are very happy to meet you!" I was inordinately pleased they spoke passable, simple English.

"So nice to meet you," Dad said, with a hearty handshake and a huge twinkle in his blue eyes, "Priyatno! Spasibo! Thank you." He was thrilled to recall a few Russian words. "Ya govoryu Rossii," he said. "I speak a little

Russian! Zovut John! Menya Ivan!" he went on. "My name is John, but you may call me Ivan!"

The two burst out laughing, and insisted they would call him "Dzhon", the closest they could get to saying "John."

Finally, I had my chance, and I reached over to shake hands with both, and Dad cut in, saying, "This is my daughter Erika; she speaks only English!"

"No problem," said Vadim. "We will have a good time with you and your daughter."

We had obviously met two decent and intelligent men, who seemed very eager to take us on the road trip that would soon become the highlight of my father's life.

They drove us to our hotel, the big international Intourist Hotel, where they helped us get checked in, and escort us to our rooms, with promises to be back at a time convenient for us next morning, when we would finally begin the most important part of this amazing journey. I learned from them that we were closer to the colonies than I expected, and that we could do a separate day trip every day from this hotel, that it was, at most about fifty kilometers southward.

Dad, even though tired and somewhat worn, was beginning to feel his spirits lifted. I could see the glow in his face. Something was hitting him about being back in his old homeland, and not wasting one moment, he said, "Before you leave us, please let us invite you to the hotel bar for a vodka; you will be our guests?" They didn't need much persuasion, and I was glad to see they were fairly westernized in their thinking. They were after all university students, so their knowledge of things was quite universal. "Nazdorovya," Dad said, as we all raised glasses. "Cheers, and thank you. Spasibo!" The two young men thoroughly enjoyed the moment, and we spent a wonderful hour getting acquainted. It was as if we had met two long-lost family members.

Aleksei was born in Kiev, a history student at the Taras Shevchenko University of Kiev, and his dream was to go on to become a historian or history professor. He told us his particular interest in Russian history was precisely the Ukraine, the evolution and development of its southern colonies, and so on. Vadim, born in Dnepropetrovsk, was a languages student, at the same university, and hoped to become an international businessman some day. We seemed to have hit upon a perfect pair, and they were both thrilled to have been given this assignment for their Summer work, telling us they would get credit for it toward their degrees. All this news made me very happy, and Dad looked over at me, with all the pride he could muster: "Daughter, you've scored gold here. Thank you. Pozhalista!"

"Nyet, nichego, it's nothing," I said. And he smiled proudly.

"How did you know what to say?"

"Well, Dad, there's a wonderful tool on the computer called Google translator. I memorized a few terms, just so I could see your proud reaction."

~ ~ ~ ~ ~ ~ ~

[Fast forwarding here to the historical event at the Lichtenau train station. We have come to a Saturday morning at breakfast. Dad, feeling somewhat weary from several days of visits to and wandering around his known villages of the Molotschna, has requested a day to rest.]

~ ~ ~ ~ ~ ~ ~

Dad and I met in our quiet little corner in the dining room for our morning coffee and some crisp bread with butter and that plum jam he loved so much. We were looking forward to a day off from traipsing around old and desolate villages. Perhaps a wander around the town's square, to see what the craftsmen and artisans of the Ukraine were making and selling.

Ready to enjoy a gentle breakfast, we both suddenly noticed a large new group of people entering, westerners by all accounts. Somewhat taken aback, I looked at Dad and went off to get a coffee refill. In the coffee line, I got curious about all the apparent excitement, people greeting people, and shaking hands vigorously, and decided to ask the gentleman behind me what was going on: "It's the eightieth year celebration tomorrow, Sunday," he said, "at the train station in Lichtenau, commemorating the people who left from there in 1924."

"Oh wow," I said, my heart definitely skipping a beat. He saw the instant expression of surprise on my face but didn't inquire, not sure why not.

"We are a very large group of Mennonites, from America, Europe, and Canada, on a Black Sea cruise, and this stop was planned to coincide with that celebration, as some of us had parents and/or grandparents who were among the refugees who fled from there. In fact," he went on to say, "a few months ago, I received a call from an elderly gentleman in Manitoba, inquiring about this cruise precisely because of the celebration in Lichtenau. He told me he was on that train with his parents when he was just a young boy." I was definitely welling up with tears from a deep and faraway place at this unbelievable coincidence, but continued to listen with focus; I already had a scheme brewing in my mind but didn't want to give anything away at this moment. "I nearly had him convinced to come with us," the gentleman continued. "It would have been such an honor; but he said he wanted to think about it and I never heard back from him. From my research, it is my belief he may well be the only one left from that exodus. I believe he was an Epp. Anyway, this group is here for the big celebration tomorrow at noon."

"Thank you, how exciting," and I smiled for more reasons than he could even have imagined. I was nearly bursting with joy, but I didn't want to divulge my secret just yet.

"By the way, my name is Jacob. Are you by chance here to join the group or the celebration?" He suddenly seemed curious.

We shook hands, "I'm Erika. And to answer your question, no on both accounts, but I am here with my ninety-year-old father, and the two of us have been traveling around the Molotschna Colony for the past few days, visiting, among other places, his birth village of Lindenau, and then Tiegerweide, where he grew up. We were actually planning to visit Lichtenau tomorrow, but I had no idea about the big event at the train station."

In fact, I truly had no idea about any of this, but suddenly it was all coming together. I could not believe the coincidence, of our visit here at the exact same time as the ceremonies at the train station. The chances of this happening as a planned meeting would have been non-existent at best. Stunned and in some disbelief, I took our coffee back to the table to tell Dad what was going on. I was also, way back in my mind, suddenly remembering the urgency in his voice when he called me in Paris to hurry home so we could get on with this journey.

The rascal! He had known about it, apparently, but he never told me until this morning, here in Zaporozhye at the Intourist Hotel, in the dining room, over morning coffee.

"Dad, were you aware of this celebration at the train station in Lichtenau?" I asked. "This group is here from North America and Europe for this occasion."

"Yes, it's what I read about many months ago," he said, with complete nonchalance, "but I wasn't interested in going with a large group on a cruise and all the rest of it. I actually called the guy at the head of the organization in Toronto, to inquire. His name was Jacob — a coordinator for Balkan and Black Sea cruises for Mennonites. Jacob heard my story, and tried to persuade me to come with them on that cruise. That's when I called you in Paris, to see if you thought we could do this alone."

"But Dad," I implored, "this is important for you. You were on that very train that left from Lichtenau in 1924. It behooves you to be part of the celebration?"

We finished our continental breakfast, and I got up and said: "Come on,

Dad. I want someone to meet you."

We went over to Jacob's table, and I said, "Excuse me, I want you to meet someone with an Epp name who called you some months ago about the Lichtenau train station celebrations. Dad, this is Jacob, and Jacob, this is my father, John Epp, the ten-year-old kid who left on that train from Lichtenau with his parents in 1924."

Jacob bolted out of his chair, and Dad nearly dropped his teeth.

"Oh for Pete's sake!" That's exactly what Dad said.

And Jacob, in absolute disbelief, with eyes as big as saucers, uttered: "You are kidding! It was you? And you got here on your own. I was telling Erika, who I now know is your daughter, about a call I received from an elderly gentleman in Manitoba, and that I had so hoped he would join the cruise and be here for the celebration. An actual living link."

Then he looked at me, "You didn't tell me! This is fantastic. We have to get you both there and make sure the media gets you into the Mennonite newspapers back home. This is wonderful!" He gave Dad a hearty handshake, calling him Mister Epp, and promised the fun had just begun. And then he left, acting like the cat that had just caught the canary for dinner.

Dad and I smiled at one another and walked back to our hotel rooms. "So, Dad, is this why you were, perhaps secretly, in a bit of a hurry to get to the Molotschna."

"You know, daughter," he confessed, "that was too many months ago, I honestly forgot. I remember reading about it, and calling Jacob, but I was suddenly just eager to visit here on my own steam. And while I was still able and ambulatory. And once I realized you and I could do this, I forgot about anything else."

~ ~ ~ ~ ~ ~ ~

The eventful Sunday was upon us. Regardless of celebrations, Lichtenau was to be the third and last village of deliberation for Dad. And as if the angels had planned it, Dad would suddenly be the major celebrant of the day. Jokingly, I polished the tips of his shoes, meaning I wiped off the dust from days of walking on gravel and dirt roads, and told him he was ready for the photojournalists. With his engaging smile, and those soulful eyes, he did not need a three-piece suit and tie for the occasion!

I took him to the dining room, to our secluded round table, and went off to get him his crusty bread with butter and plum jam, and a large pot of coffee, and told him I'd be right back. News of Dad's link to this entire occasion had already spread everywhere in the immediate vicinity. Even the hotel's registration desk employees had heard about it, so they told our two students, Aleksei and Vadim, and the excitement was moving forward full throttle. I suspected the two would already be in the lobby waiting for us by now. They loved kibitzing around with the pretty girls working behind the counter, and there they were. Adorably dressed in blue jeans and pressed white shirts, they were feeling the festive mood as well. I gave them one hundred hrivnas and said, "Aleksei and Vadim, listen carefully. Things have changed a little, as you already know. I saw a flower stand nearby on the big boulevard; please go down there and get two bouquets, a small one to place in the van for Dad, and a bigger one to give to Dad during the ceremony in Lichtenau. Ponyima? Khorosho! Spasibo! Understand? Good! Thank you!" I said. "But please hide the second bouquet in the hatch of the van until we get to the station! I will see you here in about twenty minutes, yes!"

I was feeling so happy, I gave them each a hug and they danced out of the lobby with big smiles, feeling as if they had the biggest and most important stake in this entire event.

And they did!

I went back to the dining room to join Dad, but there was no room at the table. He was suddenly surrounded by three gentlemen from the big group, one of them Jacob, who was busy asking him questions. Dad was holding forth appropriately, and didn't even notice me nearby. Jacob got up to talk with me for a minute, and I assured him Dad would be fine. "Our van is waiting for us, so we better hit the road so I can place him front row center on the train station bench prescribed for celebrants!" Jacob laughed, and agreed.

Aleksei and Vadim were in the lobby, grinning from ear to ear, waiting to load Dad into the van. I was curious as to what transpired with the flowers, but the instant they opened the van door, I could see they had had some wonderful and loving fun. There, in a slot between the two front seats, they had placed a small bouquet of little blue flowers, and I gave Vadim a wink of approval. Dad got in, noticed the flowers and wondered if this was a Sunday tradition in Ukraine? And Aleksei, just before closing the door, said: "Dzohn, they are for you! So you remember us!" A dagger went straight to my heart; how thoughtful to have found tiny blue forget-me-nots for the occasion. It was perfect, and Dad was quickly filling up with emotion and joy slightly beyond his capacity to absorb all at once. I loved the whole scene. Once Aleksei and I were in the back seat, he pointed to the other bouquet behind us in the hatch, and I whispered to him that I wanted him and Vadim to present it to Dad at the ceremony, and that they were to keep their eye on me, and I would let them know when. Their pleasure in this day defied description, and I could tell they were happy beyond belief. Aleksei, being the history student, was particularly thrilled that he was going to be part of living history in his own country. He was very proud.

~ ~ ~ ~ ~ ~ ~

We arrived in Lichtenau and it was obvious there was going to be a celebration. The colony people were already gathering at the train station. I went by quickly to check out the scene as to the bench Dad would be sitting on, and then the four of us took a stroll across the tracks behind the station, toward what looked like a goat farm. Dad bent down to touch the tracks as we crossed over, a tactile gesture to trigger his memory from eighty years ago. "This was the track along which that train was parked just long enough to fill it up with villagers from all around the colony for their immediate escape from the terror filled lands of the great Ukraine," he reminisced.

I grabbed his arm and said: "Dad, I'm so thankful these tracks got you out of here and all the way to the little two-room house on the prairie so I could be born, to bring you back here!" He smiled beautifully and proudly, and with gratitude.

As we wandered around, seeing strawpiles here and there, and a pigsty near the barn, Dad recalled reading about Lichtenau years after he had grown up in Canada. It was 1804, exactly one hundred years ago, a date that would also be highlighted here today. Lichtenau was one of the four earliest villages built and settled in the Molotschna Colony, and it was the largest, which is why the train station was built there. It was also conveniently located at the end of the middle road, where all three colony roads converged.

We could see people beginning to assemble. With Aleksei and Vadim on either side of Dad, they walked back with him to the designated area and made sure he was 'securely' seated. They then went back to the van to get the other bouquet of flowers. I saw Jacob, who motioned for Dad to move to end of the bench nearest him, and I stood behind him.

Gradually, all the villagers, friends, historians, journalists, visitors, and speakers convened, and the program got started. Jacob was the narrator; he stepped behind the podium, the audience fell silent, and I knew we would hear the big news first. He proceeded to recount the entire story of his phone conversation with Dad months ago, up to the present moment, and then, with great flourish, in Low German first, and then in English, pronounced: "Ladies and gentlemen, it is such an honor, not to mention an unbelievable privilege, to have with us here today one of the few people left from that great exodus eighty years ago, one of the passengers on the train when he was just a boy of ten. He is here with his oldest daughter, Erika. Please acknowledge the presence of John Epp, on the bench next to me." And the applause was thunderous.

Dad got up to accept it all as he bowed with grace and noble humility — the last known standing icon of an amazing life, a direct connection, to then, to today, to now.

While the applause went on for several moments, I turned around to catch the eye of either Aleksei or Vadim to bring the flowers. Aleksei carried the bouquet, and Vadim was right next to him. They went up to Dad on the bench, and presented him with the bouquet. It was so appropriate and beautiful because they were the indigenes of today. Dad was, of course, very surprised, and he had to hug both Vadim and Aleksei, and just stand there shaking his head in disbelief. Normally, Dad is a great impromptu chatterer, but this was too overwhelming for him today, so he sat down with his flowers on his lap, and waved to the crowds.

The program was short and concise, informative, and respectful. And immediately after, several media types surrounded Dad to get photographs and some bits for their newspaper columns; others just came up to shake hands and comment on the wonderful surprise. The nice thing was Dad was so surprised. This was not planned; it just happened. Spontaneity at its best. Serendipity at its most beautiful.

Dad was ignited, he told me later, and could not fathom it all. Feeling slightly out of body, a little non-plussed perhaps, he remained on his bench for a while longer while he tried to bring it all into focus, looking for clues to ally with those first ten years of his life, looking for identification to the simple joys he experienced as a precocious boy born and raised in this vast country. It was his moment of closure. He was the perfect monument, where history, place, and circumstance were in perfect collusion in their proclamation of the historical event of the departure of many hundreds of original Mennonite settlers from this area in 1924.

~ ~ ~ ~ ~ ~ ~

I wrote some prose into my journal that evening, of my observations of Dad, and from remarks from him throughout the past days:

For My Father.

what does it all mean?
birthplace and boyhood
final visiting place and manhood

distant memories of joyful adventures
mysteries
poverty
curiosities

worries

cruel histories of ruthless moments
temporary togetherness
departures
separations

questions
broken dreams

new revelations
old confirmations

fathers and great-grandmothers
toil and sweat

indefatigable inhabitants
some old and grizzled
with fingers bent and bony

garden plots left behind
and kurgan mounds growing
soldiers and sadness
cruelty and lives taken
revolutions lost
battles won
miles and miles of cemeteries

broken churches
crumbled rooftops

old brick factories
pasts echoing through gaping windowless holes

remnants of collective farms and common kitchens
pretty homes with inviting edifices and cheery blue windows

tethered goats
gaggles of geese
taunting roosters
red cows

rambling forests and rose shrubs
endless old buggy paths

acacias
creeks
hills
rivers and streams
and breathless vistas

fantasy visions of Cossacks and Tatars

Molotschna
now a new memory for you to pack in your carry-on
but with a different face
a full circle
a more comprehensive feeling
sounds of boisterous new generations and incorrigible cheer

a rich past
with an even richer future
a new hope
a continuation

Never an End

~ ~ ~ ~ ~ ~ ~

A big journey had come to its end, and Dad had been patient though some things were still unresolved in his heart. He had questions, and he found a few answers, he had lived into the present day with the answers. I slid a long prose poem underneath his hotel room door that evening. I tried to speak in his person.

I.
i try to understand
it was different then
there was a virginal faith
an unlikely hope
an unprecedented trust

things thrived here once
my mother sang and cooked borscht
my father planted fields that grew full and luxuriant
i and my siblings and cousins skipped about playfully
swam in meandering streams
squealed happily in and out of the school house

II.
then wars and revolutions blew everything sideways
it was 1924 for some
mothers fearful grabbed some food and clothing
fathers apprehensive grabbed their children
all headed quickly and quietly for a train station
sadly awaiting departures to foreign lands
certainly not vacation lands

III.
a whole world
an entire life of innocent joy and consistent fulfillment
renounced
left behind
abandoned in complete surrender

homes standing back in shock at our abrupt departure
desolate and forlorn
left in sudden unwanted stillness
overlooking ghostly landscapes
empty wooden food bowls left behind on makeshift wooden eating tables

IV.
it might as well have been a play
ending its first act on a theatre stage
actors temporarily out of sight
behind the scenes to give room for a set change

V.
whirring by on a new train this day
eighty years later
visits to battlefields now cemeteries
visits to past villages now memorials
i try to realize the meaning of our disrupted history
try to reconcile on their behalf with unnecessary infringement
evil-mongers and sedition
lawless intruders and excessive infliction
malintentioned insurgents and torture
moons broken and suns shattered

i try to understand the reasons for such destruction
    chaotic havoc
    pernicious ruin
    egomaniacal disarray

— the reason is imperialist selfishness

i try to understand why things needed to be so broken
*   leaving them for uncorrupted believers to be built up again*
*   — the reason is supremacist selfishness*

i try to understand the meaning of justification for so much meddlesome
invasion
*   for fraudulent slogans passing for solutions*
*   — the reason is despotic selfishness*

VI.
it is still the same landscape
peaceful now
with mirrored ponds
wholesome gardens
white egrets dunking for moss
storks clacking their beaks
and competing for nesting rites atop steep poles and granary rooftops

VII.
how was it in my child's mind eighty long years ago
all things half seen
half heard
perhaps where darkness loomed in my father's mind
i saw a big train machine come to a hissing stop
to give me a happy ride
perhaps where sadness clouded my mother's heart
i experienced miracles in my child's mind
sleeping on cushions of cardboard
the adventure was indifferent to my pleasure
and the destination pointless to my curiosity

was there excitement?
did i see road signs?
was i scared?
did i dream about a future?
did i wonder?

VIII.
did i feel i was becoming someone?

~ ~ ~ ~ ~ ~ ~

Dad and I returned home from this amazing journey, safely and in one piece. I was grateful for every day with him throughout these past few weeks. I felt so privileged to have escorted him with his high hopes on this journey to Molotschna Colony, a journey that for him meant returning to the place of his birth, and coming full circle. It was a spacious vista, perhaps visually empty of many buildings and streams and objects he remembered, but inexpressibly filled with memories for him. Between the steppes and the wide blue air, he was there.

Dad's name is etched in his village forever; it's there. He saw it, and I saw him see it, albeit through salty tears; nonetheless, it is there. Memories of beautiful drives from village to village are there, all of them forming a dynamic and powerful collage of indelible images.

Collectively, they have settled themselves upon my own mind like eternal dust.

ACKNOWLEDGMENTS

My heartfelt thanks, first and foremost, to Sean Owens, who germinated the seed for this entire project, and ultimately led it from public readings to printed form. Encouraging at every turn, his necessary and enlightened guidance have made this first time around a very rewarding process.

Across the radar beams and through the articulate channels of Michael Welch, I was empowered with consistent confidence.

The constant and loving encouragement of Joseph d'Antonio and Marlowe Hyer was unwavering and so appreciated.

Countless years of inspired mentorship from Cathleen Gallander taught me that a life simply but solidly begun can end in wonderful growth and personal gain.

For nearly half a century, I have been thankful for the absolute and creative inspiration of my dear friend in southwest France, the artist and painter, Bruno Bieth.

Though they are sadly no longer on the planet, I am grateful to my parents, John Epp and Katherine Engbrecht, for conspiring to bring me to life, and to my sisters, Ruth Rempel and Katherine Epp, for being curious alongside.

An unvarnished and unquestionable thank you to Larry Eilenberg, who for so many years provided me with a much-appreciated literary awareness.

A wrap-around aquarian hug for Agatha Doerksen, my irrefutable visionary and loving muse.

Profound gratitude to Cameron Eng, the indisputable internet wrangler, who successfully converted me to the wonders of a personal website.

Through her unique lifestyle and enviable writing, Eva Hayward unknowingly infused me with courage and confidence in the art of written expression.

I am indebted to Gabor Beszeda, Jacob Brownwood, and Willem Vonk, for being my character stand-ins.

I am tremendously grateful to Exit Theatre's Artistic Director, Christina Augello, for offering me this rewarding opportunity, and to Managing

Director, Richard Livingston, for being the stalwart soldier of the EXIT Press providing endless and valuable assistance.

My sincere thanks to Gail Goldman for her time and worthy counsel, and to Happy Hyder for emboldened artwork on the cover.

A giant thank you to Zoë Inman for her enthusiastic generosity and invitation to do a reading in her home.

I am honored to acknowledge my many devoted and loving friends, who appear here as the abecedarian menagerie: Teagle Bougere, whose enthusiasm for my writing never ceased; Jacob Brownwood, whose inspired wonder for life kept me buoyant; Victoria Dadam, who saw the finished project before it began; Helen Foli, my oldest living confidante; Jonathan Huxley, who believed in me and challenged me way beyond limits; Mark Jackson, who added rich dimensions to my self-esteem; Gilles Jéronymos, who was the lighthouse from afar; and Judd Kleinman, whose insistence was invaluable. Alexandra de Malcolm provided light and ardor from Paris; Matthew Martin watched me grow up and helped me through all of it; Jean-François Pauly was the consistent and energetic spark of my 'other home'; John Powers always followed closely with endless caring and warmth; Nikita Schoen was a quietly driving force behind this process; Cat Stevans brought fire from the heart; Jerry Walker infused me with vital belief; and Kathryn Wood became my secret beneficiary.

I am finally immensely grateful to the many who subsidized me in spirit: Allie Aluchi, Dirk Bender, Geraldine de Braune, Baptiste Caraux, Keith Coleman, Brian DeFehr, Randall Friesen, Andrew Gentile, Max Kelly, Mai Lovaas, Min Matson, John McCadden, Alexandros Pagonis, Uwe Pflug, Martin Rogriguez, James Saidy, Allen Throolin, Sibylle Tobler, Linda Wang, Shirley Westerhoff, Barrie Wiggins, Brad Wilson, James Wadsworth, Miguel Zavala, and Aleksandra Zawicka.

AUTHOR

Erika Atkinson was born on the prairies of central Canada, in southern Manitoba, into a family of penurious Russian Mennonite immigrants. There she spent her childhood and young adulthood until age eighteen. Having little interest in formal higher education, she instead began preparing to join the Canadian Foreign Service. She came to Washington, D.C., via Ottawa, Canada, a journey that became the ignition point of her travel interests. She lived and worked as an academic administrative assistant in schools, colleges, and universities in Canada, the United States, and Europe. Now long retired from the nine-to-five, she continues to expand her archive of travels and travel experiences. She lives happily in San Francisco's Castro neighborhood.

EXIT Press

EXIT Press is the publishing division of EXIT Theatre, a San Francisco theater company that was founded in 1983. Published books include *Ten Plays* by Mark Jackson, *Snakes of Kampuchea* by Mark Knego, *Practical Tales For Children and other stories* by Mark Romyn, and *Woyzeck, Pelleas and Melisande, Ubu Roi* translated by Rob Melrose. Coming soon is *Songs of Hestia: Five Plays From the 2010 Olympians Festival.*

CPSIA information can be obtained at www.ICGtesting.com
Printed in the USA
LVOW050455180612

286550LV00002B/56/P